Solving The
Retirement
Puzzle
With
4 Easy Pieces

Solving The Retirement Puzzle With 4 Easy Pieces

Peter R. Wechsler | Jeremy A. Wechsler, Esq.

SOLVING THE RETIREMENT PUZZLE WITH 4 EASY PIECES

ABOUT THIS BOOK

We really hadn't thought of writing a book. Since neither father nor son had ever written a book before, we weren't sure where to start. After about the 16th time I heard from clients that we needed to put our wisdom down on paper, I thought that would take up about three pages. Go figure: it's actually enough to fill a real book.

Jeremy and I pondered over lunch one day whether sharing our knowledge of retirement, income and estate planning for middle income folks made sense. Would our common sense approach resonate for those close to, or already in, retirement? Based on all the great feedback we were constantly getting from our clients, we decided to put pen to paper.

After talking with clients and friends about what kind of book they'd like to see, the general consensus was to keep it short, sweet and to the point. No legalese, no financial jargon over the heads of most folks— just good sound advice, presented in an easy-to-understand way.

We wrote this book ourselves. No professionals and no ghost writers. It's not meant to be technical and it's written in a conversational style. You'll notice we've taken some liberty in the points we emphasize, along with our grammar and punctuation. My ninth grade English teacher at Central High, Mr. Weisberg, would not be too happy with my taking so much literary license. Then again, he wasn't too impressed with my writing skills back in the day.

We could have written a 300-page manuscript, but who would read it? Instead, these hundred and some pages are meant to be a guide for those lacking an overall basic understanding of retirement and estate issues. This book is designed so you can jump to the sections that most appeal to you.

As you read through the book, it is important that you watch for words, phrases, concepts or concerns that you've never heard before, or never discussed with your current financial advisor. Every day, we deal with myths and misconceptions that retirees have about financial, income and retirement planning.

If you read about some concepts in this book that are new to you, find an expert who can help you interpret what you read here, and how it can be applied to your retirement plan. Even better, perhaps you should set up a meeting with us, and go through our Four-Step Discovery Review Process. It's complimentary and there is no obligation.

Why do people seek the help of retirement and estate specialists? Truthfully, a totally different set of skills is needed for retirement planning and distribution than most stock brokers possess, as they are mostly (supposedly) experts in accumulation—helping you get to the *Promised Land* called retirement. Then it's time to move to income and estate planning experts... or what I like to call *decumulation* experts. I'm not sure it's a word yet, but you get the idea.

If you find this book helpful, pass it on to your friends and family. Since most people don't have the knowledge about income and estate planning, alert your friends by email to get a copy, or even better, buy a few extra copies and give them as presents to your friends, siblings and kids. Most important, get this information to those you know will soon be retiring, or are recently retired. Most people are afraid to ask for help or don't know where to go. You can help them. That's what friends are for!

Peter R. Wechsler

P.S.—I'd be remiss if I didn't mention my grandfather, Bernie Plotkin. As a men's haberdasher, he taught me one of the most important lessons about providing superior customer and client services. In the mens' clothing business, you made or lost money for the year based on sales from Thanksgiving to Christmas. Gramps told me one time that he had to provide great service all year long, because if he lost one customer a week, he'd have 50 less customers over Christmas. I couldn't have been more than 10 years old at the time, but that lesson has guided me throughout my professional career.

Note: The information in this book is correct to the best of our knowledge and as of the publication date. Laws and products are subject to change and you should always consult with a competent professional prior to making investment decisions. Individual situations can vary; therefore, the information should be relied upon when coordinated with individual professional advice.

CONTENTS

CHAPTER ONE
Where Have All The Pensions Gone?

As an early '50s-born baby boomer, I am definitely a product of 60s folk music, and a lifelong Peter, Paul, and Mary fan. As I wrote the chapter title, I couldn't help recalling the song *Where Have All the Flowers Gone?* According to the lyrics, the flowers went to graveyards. Guess that's post-retirement planning, and not the subject of this book. Let's get started, and together we'll solve the retirement puzzle.

First, a little history and a little perspective. Following the Great Depression of the 1930s and until 1974, America had a retirement system that worked rather well. It was a system where many workers didn't worry too much about their retirement. They weren't concerned about financial markets and they knew very little about Wall Street.

First off, many people figured they'd only live a few years after retirement. When Social Security began in 1935, the average person was only expected to live to age 62. Not a long retirement before taking that last limo ride.

Second, many folks were guaranteed a secure retirement income from their employer. It was called a pension and it came along with the gold watch. Those who had retired and those about to retire anticipated, with confidence, that their income from Social Security and a pension would be adequate.

"Simple," "consistent," "steady" and "worry-free" were words my grandfather used when he talked about the retirement system of yesteryear. There was no need for credentialed financial planners or stockbrokers. In fact, it was a retirement system where the employee was not responsible for any of the investment decisions. The lack of financial anxiety was a great benefit of the old system.

Your parent's pensions were very predictable and provided the security of knowing exactly what their retirement benefit would be from the time they started with the company or the government until the year they retired. They were given a statement each year with this information. In this defined-benefit plan, retirees received a monthly pension check guaranteed for the rest of their lives. Employees knew how much they would receive, thus, the term "defined." Thinking back to those days, I like to call this "mailbox money."

There were no IRA or 401(k) plans during this period. If retirees wanted to further supplement their income, they used tax-deferred annuities, issued and guaranteed through insurance companies. They'd just call up their life insurance agent and, before long, they had secured more retirement income. Retirement security was never so simple.

Defined Benefit Pension Plans— The Post-Depression Pension Plan
Let's call defined pension plans "your parent's pension," since fewer and fewer of today's workers are retiring with a pension. Until 1974, the pension plan was the primary retirement system in the United States. There were substantial benefits for the employee in terms of security and guarantees, and far less anxiety and worries about financial matters than I see today.

Why'd The System Work So Well?
From the day you began working for the company, you knew what to expect in 40 years upon retirement. Talk about instant security— there was no guessing about whether you'd be able to retire with lifetime income.

You also knew your pension plan was being professionally managed.

The personnel manager didn't manage the investments. Instead, this was done by a highly educated, experienced and professional pension management team. Pension managers, anticipating the needs of future employees, could look at an investment timeline as far out as 100 years.

Risk was greatly reduced due to economies of scale, since there were often hundreds even thousands of employees claiming ownership to a fraction of the total pension pie. Each year, the pension managers could plan for the number of retirements that year and make certain to have enough liquidity.

From the 1940s to the early 1970s, the Depression was still fairly fresh in everybody's mind. Although businesses still wanted to take care of their employees and provide them with the safety and security of a pension, they also wanted to remove themselves from the risk of paying out that pension for the next 20 to 30 years, or longer. So pension managers turned to the only solution available.

The company couldn't give the money to the bank, because a bank doesn't have the ability to provide guaranteed lifetime income. Neither could they give the employees' pension money to Wall Street, because Wall Street doesn't have the ability to guarantee a pension for life.

So who did they turn to? Life insurance companies—the one group of companies that everybody loves to hate. Pension managers turned over the lump sum of money to life insurance companies in order to create the guaranteed pension for as long as the employee lived.

Why Did Business Turn to Life Insurance Companies?
I know, I know – we all hate insurance companies. Two of the most hated terms in the English language are "Life Insurance" and "Annuities". That being said, life insurance companies are in the business of guarantees. The insurance industry knows how to provide both guarantees at death (life insurance) and guarantees for longevity (pension annuities or income annuities).

I know you won't believe this, but insurance companies are businesses of integrity, not greed (even though they have all the money). I can already hear you: *what about AIG?* It wasn't the insurance side of the business that got into trouble, and all claims were paid promptly.

Policyholders may never get rich, but they do sleep well at night. This is what American businesses wanted for their employees back then, and it's what Congress wanted for Americans after the Depression.

Today, millions of Americans know their pensions will be deposited directly into their checking accounts every month. They have absolutely no concerns about safety and security. Nor do they have a need to watch CNBC all day, gasping for breath every time the Dow drops 100 points. Every month, the pension arrives on time and will for the rest of their lives. The life insurance company system of retirement works!

What Changed?
The late 1960s and early 1970s were pretty dismal times on Wall Street. Congress became concerned about the health and viability of the big Wall Street firms. Financial markets were weak and solutions were needed to regain consumer trust. Along came discounted brokerage fees and no-load mutual funds.

But Wall Street was still hurting. So where did they turn? Congress, of course! Your lobbying dollars at work!

In 1974, after extensive lobbying by Wall Street and large businesses, Congress enacted new retirement laws for Americans known today as ERISA, the Employee Retirement Income Security Act. There were many parts to the ERISA law, but two were critical.

First, the vesting rules for "your parents' pension plan" changed. In the old days, you needed to work for the same company almost your entire career to receive your pension. But ERISA changed the vesting rules so you could leave the company along the way and still get your prorated pension before normal retirement age. This drove the pension managers crazy. They needed to restructure portfolio investments because benefits needed to mature earlier. With shorter time horizons, investments needed to change, causing diminished returns.

The second noteworthy aspect of ERISA was that it ushered in the Do-It-Yourself (DIY) retirement system, better known as the Individual Retirement Account (IRA). This "defined contribution system" would now cause Americans to learn how to invest for retirement on their own.

Who would help financially uneducated American workers with these new laws? Wall Street!

Who was desperate to find a new niche opportunity to expand their markets? Wall Street!

Who had the financial solutions employees would need? Wall Street!

Wall Street couldn't have been happier – for about a minute. The Street figured out that, given the option, retirement savers would naturally choose the security of a bank or an insurance company to grow their savings. These choices would cut into Wall Street fees, since most retirees would choose guarantees over promises with no guarantees.

So, what did Wall Street do? Again, the Street lobbied Congress.

The Birth of the 401(k)
Beginning on January 1, 1980, Wall Street found its answer to becoming the gatekeeper of the American workers retirement savings with the 401(k) plan. By 1986, 401(k) plans had become very popular after Congress tweaked some of the non-discrimination rules in the original 401(k) bill.

We all know the rest of the story. Pensions began to disappear. New technology companies stayed away from these defined benefit plans as many older, mature companies began to freeze their pension plans and move to 401(k) plans.

The outcome of "The Great Retirement Experiment," which started with ERISA in 1974, is that fewer Americans have enough savings to retire comfortably. On top of that, they now need to decide how to manage their 401(k) and IRA accounts to last for 30 to 35 year retirements. It has become painfully clear that the cost of retirement is far higher than anyone could have predicted in the past.

"Inflation" is the key word here. Having worked with retirees for more than a decade, I see clearly that retirees are in denial about the effects of inflation (we'll cover that in Chapter 3). It is evident that America is headed for a severe social problem, probably the worst to ever affect our aging population in the history of our country.

As a retirement planning specialist, my goal is to make certain that you have a safe, inflation-adjusted income plan that is guaranteed to never run out of money, no matter how long you (and your spouse) live. None of us can control what happens out in the big, bad world, but we can control what happens in our personal world. Helping folks sleep well at night is my overriding mission.

So What's the Bottom Line?
First, congratulations! You made it through the first chapter. I promise future chapters will be more interesting.

Second, the big takeaway from this chapter is that with 401(k)s, 403(b)s and deferred compensation plans, along with IRAs, retirees today must take personal responsibility for their retirement income. If you're lucky enough to get a pension, you are ahead of the game today! But odds are, you have also probably stashed away money into your IRA accounts, and you will need to decide how to invest, grow and protect that nest egg. Let the fun begin!

CHAPTER TWO
Risk and the Rule of 100

What is your *Risk Tolerance?* What's your *Risk Comfort Level?* How much risk do you have in your portfolio? Most folks don't even know.

I am amazed at how often I sit down with a retiree, or someone close to retirement, to discuss risk and find out that they have no idea how much risk they really have. They generally have no idea what their real rate of return has been on their entire nest egg over the past five or ten years.

I love it when people tell me they have a low-risk portfolio, only to find that 75% or more of their retirement assets are subject to the ups and downs of the market. Even better is when I'm told how their broker characterizes their portfolio as "low risk." Folks, risk is risk! When the market tanks, there is nowhere to hide.

Prudential Insurance had a great marketing campaign, which was right on the money. Called the Red Zone, Prudential says the five years before retirement and the five years after retirement are the most critical to preserving your nest egg, so it lasts longer than you do. A severe market decline in those years, and your entire plan can go up in smoke, and you too can be a greeter at Walmart. Not to worry; they now let you stand on thick mats.

So What Is This Rule of 100?
Even if they know how much risk they have in their portfolio, most retirees have no idea what's an appropriate amount of risk to have.

The Rule of 100 is a good starting point. Subtract your age from 100, and this is the approximate amount of your investable assets you should have at risk in the market.

For example, let's say you just turned 65.

Rule of:	100
Less Age:	-65
Amount of Risk:	35%

Say you have $700,000 in investable assets, and you've just celebrated your 70th birthday. How much money should you have in risk? Using the Rule of 100, a good starting amount to have at risk would be $210,000, while leaving $490,000 safe. See how simple this stuff is?

Your Risk vs. Your Values
Discussing risk is always an interesting conversation. I can't tell you how often I sit down with a couple and the first thing they tell me is how conservative they are. They cut coupons, only buy what's on sale and never turn on the air conditioner until it's about 90 degrees in the house. Trust me, I know about the air conditioner from my days when I did lots of house calls.

But is that conservatism consistent? Not when these same retirees have 60, 70 or 80% of their investable assets at risk to the market. Their values don't match up with their investment portfolio.

What's your approach to risk?

Are you still trying to hit home runs in the stock market? Would a better approach be to hit singles and doubles, since we know the homerun hitters often have the most strikeouts?

Just so you know, I am not a sports person, so pardon the analogy. I was always the last one to be chosen when playing wiffle ball or half ball in the driveway. Since I couldn't throw a ball straight, it's no wonder my dad called me "dead eye." They always stuck me in the outfield. When I got bored out there, usually around the third inning, I'd just get on my bike and ride off into the sunset. That drove my brother Roger nuts.

Most of my clients are middle-income people. Hard workers, who also worked hard to accumulate assets for retirement. So a good starting point is the Rule of 100. The amount you should have at risk depends on many factors—including your lifestyle, your pension income (if so fortunate), your age and the age of your spouse (if married).

What's at Risk in Your Portfolio?
No doubt stocks and mutual funds are at risk to the ups and downs of the market. So are ETFs (Exchange Traded Funds), UITs (Unit Investment Trusts) and REITs (Real Estate Investment Trusts).

Numerous clients of mine worked for General Electric (GE). They are the most loyal company people I ever met, and many still hold big blocks of GE stock in their portfolio. So let's look at this company's stock price history. In 2000, GE stock hit $60 per share. In early 2009, the stock traded as low as $6.75. As I write this chapter in April 2017, GE stock is sitting at $29.64 a share.

Think about it: this stock is 58% below its high 15 years ago. Not too pretty, but better than where it was in March 2009, when it was 89% below its high.

From a tax-planning perspective, you'd be much better off if your GE stock was held in your non-IRA accounts versus in an IRA. That's because you could have sold shares of GE and taken a big tax loss, which you could offset against future market gains. If it's in an IRA, you have no ability to harvest the losses. You just pay taxes on every last dime you pull out of your IRA, whether or not you ever made money on the holding because what was invested were pre-tax dollars.

When we talk about GE, we're not talking about just any old company. We're talking about one of the premier worldwide companies of all time. General Electric: they bring good things to life. Perhaps so... but not if you have been an investor for the past 15 years.

What About Bonds and Bond Funds?
I'll try to summarize here. An entire book could be written on bonds and bond funds. In fact, many books have been.

As I pen these words, interest rates are at historic lows. In fact, we have watched interest rates go down for the past thirty years. Remember those CDs you bought in 1980 at 15% or 16%? I still have clients fondly recalling those days and still waiting to latch on to those rates again, but this time they want 15- or 20-year maturities. Lots of luck!

What you need to know about bonds is the inverse relationship to interest rates. With interest rates at historic lows, can they go any lower? Forget the toaster, soon banks are going to start charging storage fees to hold your money.

So what happens when interest rates finally start going up? The value of bonds will go down. Counter-intuitive, but that's what happens. If you hold your individual bonds until maturity, you'll get back the face value of the bonds. Need to cash them in early in a rising-rate environment? You'll probably lose money on the bond.

What If Interest Rates Go Up?

INTEREST RATE / BOND PRICE RELATIONSHIP

You bought a bond for $1,000. Now let's suppose that later that year, interest rates in general go up. If new bonds costing $1,000 are paying an 8% coupon ($80 a year in interest), buyers will be reluctant to pay you face value ($1,000) for your 7% ABC bond. In order to sell, you'd have to offer your bond at a lower price – a discount – that would enable it to generate approximately 8% to the new owner.

In this case, that would mean a price of about $875.

What about bond funds? Even worse! With individual bonds, you are in the driver's seat. You decide when to liquidate and whether to take a loss or hold on to the bond until it matures. But with bond funds, you are at the mercy of all the other owners of that bond fund. If there are too many redemption requests, the bond fund will need to sell bonds before they mature, often at a loss in a rising interest rate environment.

What about municipal bonds? That's a "whole 'nother talk show," as they say. With states and municipalities in bad shape, there is fear of default. So far, there have not been enough defaults to spook the markets, and the yields are good on individual muni bonds. As for muni bond funds, the same losses as corporate or treasury bonds could happen down the road.

So, are individual bonds held to maturity at risk? A little, depending on their ratings. Bond funds? Yes, they are very much at risk in the future.

Are Variable Annuities at Risk?
This is a conversation I hate having, because many people have been led to believe that Variable Annuities are risk free.

While Variable Annuities have a place in the financial planning world, for many people close to retirement or in retirement, Variable Annuities should be looked at with caution. If you are in your 40s or maybe early 50s, in a high income bracket and already maxed out on your 401(k) and IRA contributions, a tax-deferred variable might make sense.

Are you close to retirement? In retirement? In that Red Zone we talked about earlier? If you answered yes to any of these, you may not be a good candidate for a Variable Annuity.

There are two main problems with these instruments. First are the high fees. The average Variable Annuity I look at has fees close to 4% per year, including rider fees and sub-account fees.

Second, since your money is invested in mutual funds, your money is at risk. Yes, you can buy principal protection riders along with other riders, but your fees will be sky high and you pay those fees every year, whether the market is up or down. We recently looked at a Variable Annuity with annual fees of 4.3%. Ouch! Oh, and just remember to read ALL the fine print. These annuities are often extremely confusing.

What are sub-account fees, you ask? They are the fees on the mutual funds inside the Variable Annuity. That's right, you are in the market, you are taking the risk and paying high fees.

Suze Orman wrote in her book, *The Road to Wealth*, about Variable Annuities. She was asked the question: "My financial advisor is recommending I buy a Variable Annuity in my retirement account. What should I do?" Suzie's answer: "Get yourself another financial advisor, pronto!"

Do you have stocks, mutual funds, bonds, bond funds, or Variable Annuities? If you need assistance with finding out if these line up with your true risk level, feel free to schedule a visit with us, and we'll sort it out together.

Market Cycles and Japan 40,000

Why do we even care about the Rule of 100 when solving the retirement puzzle? As we age, our time horizon narrows. Once we retire, we enter the protection and preservation phase of our lives and leave behind the accumulation phase.

Seldom do I meet a retiree who can't wait to lose 40 or 50% of their portfolio to market risk, just so they can go back to work. Sure, it's tough to be home with the wife all day, but really, do you want to stock shelves at Toys"R"Us?

Historically, markets have gone through long up and down cycles. We can go back a hundred years and see where the market flips every 17 to 22 years. The last lengthy bull market in the U.S. ran from 1982 to 2000, when the tech bubble burst.

If history holds true, we have several years to go before the next true bull market begins. But then again, who knows? Sure we've had several substantial ups and downs since 2000, but after 15 years, the market – adjusted for inflation – hasn't grown very much. What we never know is if a market rally is the start of the next bull market or just a bear market trap.

Bullish investors argue with me all the time, especially when I talk about market cycles. That's because most of us baby-boomers started investing in the early '80s, just as the market began its best 18-year cycle in the history of the markets. We still can't believe that this down cycle could last so long.

When all else fails, I bring up Japan. In 1989, the Nikkei 225 hit a high just shy of 40,000. At the close of 2016, the Japanese equivalent of the Dow Jones Industrial Average was sitting at just over 19,000. Twenty-six years later! Still down, and not just by a few percentage points. Twenty-seven years later, the Nikkei 225 is down over 60% from its high in 1989.

Could this happen here in the United States? Let's hope not. A 60% correction from its 2016 close of 19,762 would give us a Dow Jones Industrial Average of around 7,904. Although this is unlikely, it's still a scary thought.

What caused the Japanese market to tank? Most analysts say there were three main factors. First, they had a real estate bubble burst. Hmm, sound familiar? Seems like we are still dealing with the effects of our real estate bubble-burst, now almost eight years old.

Second, they had an aging population, as we do now. Japan was about 20 years ahead of us, but with all our baby boomers now retiring, we're catching up quick. Why does this matter?

When people retire, they are no longer working, earning a paycheck and investing in their 401(k)s, 403(b)s and IRAs. Instead, they begin to tap into their retirement accounts. As they pull money from their stocks and mutual funds, they cause a supply-demand imbalance, which can cause stock prices to ultimately drop.

An aging population is what happened in Japan and what appears to be happening here in the good old U.S. of A. One big difference: Japan is a rather closed society that doesn't let in many immigrants. And while both the U.S. and Japan have a low birth rate, the number of immigrants in the U.S. that are paying into Social Security and Medicare are helping keep those direct deposits flowing into the checking accounts of retirees. I know this can sound controversial, but it's based off the findings of numerous noted economists.

So Remind Me Again... Why Is the Rule of 100 So Important?
In retirement, you need to make certain you don't have more money exposed to the market than you can afford to lose.

The Rule of 100 is just a starting point. It's not the gospel, but it is a good place to begin. Suppose you are 70. According to the Rule of 100, you should have no more than 30% of your money exposed to the ups and downs of the market.

Many factors can alter the case for this number, including your standard of living, whether you get pensions, have rental income or high medical bills. What's most important is to know your level of risk exposure and make certain it ties in with your values and your comfort level.

Feel you might have too much risk in your portfolio? Maybe it's time to get a second opinion. Think about this, when do we generally get second opinions? Yup, when you don't like your doctor's prognosis. What I tell folks is that if you get a second opinion for your health, why not your wealth?

We love giving second opinions. Contact us if you think that makes sense.

CHAPTER THREE
Will You Outlive Your Money?
Building a Solid Income Foundation

With so many people leaving the workforce without pensions, income planning has become the most critical factor facing retirees. Even with a pension, serious issues often need to be addressed.

If married, what decision do you make concerning the spousal survivor benefit? If your pension doesn't provide for a cost of living adjustment, how will you keep pace with inflation? If you have not yet begun taking your pension, do you have any flexibility concerning when you turn on the pension and will the benefit grow the longer you wait to start?

Why is income planning so important today? Two words: Inflation and Longevity.

According to the U.S. Census Bureau, the average person retires around age 62 and lives for another 18 years. These are just averages, with many being forced to retire before 60 and others working into their 70s.

In fact, I am always quite careful when I discuss *averages*. As Mr. Lucash taught us in 10th grade biology, if you put one foot into a bucket of boiling water and the other foot into a bucket of ice water, on *average* you would be comfortable.

While we're on averages, here's another one according to some recent studies. For a 65-year-old couple today, there is over a 50% chance that at least one will live past age 92. So what's the implication when discussing income planning? With the average person retiring at 62, and with a good shot at reaching 90 or more, we as income planners need to deal with 20, 30 or 40 year retirements without a bi-weekly paycheck.

Why Worry About Inflation?
The most common set of blinders I see when discussing retirement planning, is the effects of inflation on income needs over a 20- or 30-year span. Even using a 3% inflation factor often proves difficult to comprehend and compute for those planning to retire, as well as for those who have already done so. We're often using 2.5%, keeping in mind that the Social Security average cost of living increase over the past 30 years is running around that number.

You will see in the chart on the next page how future inflation will affect a recent retiree. Look at how their income needs to grow to keep pace with just 3% inflation. Notice the chart cuts off at age 92. Guess why? We know we're living longer, but for most folks living past age 92, they're not spending that much money on food, clothing, entertainment or travel.

In fact, most retirees spend the most in their earliest years of retirement, and if in good health, many of my clients are still traveling extensively into their 80s, still buying new cars and still wintering in Florida.

For most of us, I find that ages 60 to 75 are the honeymoon years of retirement, or what I call the GO-GO YEARS, 75 to 85 the SLOW GO YEARS, and 85 on up, the NO-GO YEARS. That being the case, inflation generally becomes less of an issue starting in your mid 80s.

WILL YOUR INCOME KEEP PACE WITH INFLATION?			
YEAR	AGE	INFLATION ADJUSTMENT AT 3%	TOTAL ANNUAL INFLATION ADJUSTED INCOME NEEDED
2016	64	1,800	61,800
2017	65	1,854	63,654
2018	66	1,910	65,564

2019	67	1,967	67,531
2020	68	2,026	69,556
2021	69	2,087	71,643
2022	70	2,149	73,792
2023	71	2,214	76,006
2024	72	2,280	78,286
2025	73	2,349	80,635
2026	74	2,419	83,054
2027	75	2,492	85,546
2028	76	2,566	88,112
2029	77	2,643	90,755
2030	78	2,723	93,478
2031	79	2,804	96,282
2032	80	2,888	99,171
2033	81	2,975	102,146
2034	82	3,064	105,210
2035	83	3,156	108,367
2036	84	3,251	111,618
2037	85	3,349	114,966
2038	86	3,449	118,415
2039	87	3,552	121,968
2040	88	3,659	125,627
2041	89	3,769	129,395
2042	90	3,882	133,277
2043	91	3,998	137,276
2044	92	4,118	141,394

Sources of Retirement Income

My practice mostly revolves around middle-income folks who were savers. Most never made the big bucks, but they were conservative, a few even frugal. The result is a nice retirement nest egg, after hitting that time clock for the very last time.

So you've got the gold watch, had the retirement luncheon, packed up all your personal effects, turned in your badge and keys, and headed off into retirement. Mazel tov!

Where will the income come from? The usual suspects are:
- Social Security
- Pension(s)
- Dividends and Interest
- Rental Income
- IRA RMDs
- Annuity Income
- Part-Time Work

As income planning specialists, we need to examine and assign a realistic, conservative growth rate to each pot of money, taking into consideration that each type of account works differently. To do this, the first task is to break down your IRAs and 401(k)s into one pot, your Roth IRAs into a second pot and the rest of your investable assets into the third pot. Once we do that, we can begin to do some preliminary income planning.

What's All This Talk About Longevity Insurance?

Retirees are scared of running out of money and fear not having enough income, should they live to a ripe old age. There are some folks that talk about how they plan to run out of money at the same time they plan to run out of time. What happens if they miscalculate? Good luck with that one. Then there are those who tell me they plan to cut it really close, so close they hope the check to the funeral home bounces! Probably the same folks with the bumper sticker proclaiming *I'm Spending My Kids Inheritance*!

Then there was a couple in their early 60s who came to see me, knowing I wasn't a miracle worker. They had figured out they were not in very good shape to retire but at least they had a plan. They figured if they took late retirements and early deaths, they'd just about squeeze by. Not the best plan I ever heard, but I give them credit. It was a plan!

Leave it to the insurance companies to come up with a solution so you never run out of money. Today we call it Longevity Insurance. Using either Variable Annuities or Fixed Indexed Annuities (sometimes called Indexed Annuities, FIAs or Hybrid Annuities), you can ensure lifetime guaranteed income (based on the claims paying ability of the issuer) for you and your spouse, if married. In effect, we are creating a pension for you and your spouse.

Oops! I forgot to tell you we were about to discuss what seems to be just about the most hated word in the English language... *Annuities*. And in case you're wondering, the two most hated words in the English language, *Life Insurance*, will be along soon enough. And not to be outdone, we'll follow it up with the three most hated words... *Long Term Care*. Maybe this is why I got such a great reaction at my recent high school reunion when people asked what I did for a living.

The truth is that most folks want and need an annuity, but not if it's called an annuity. Go figure! So us creative types came up with Longevity Insurance. Now folks love it!

For a small fee, ranging from .75% to .95% per year, your annuity can become a guaranteed stream of income you can't outlive. Today we are using annuities where the income value grows at 7% per year until you decide to begin taking income. Think about it: here is a way to take a portion of your investible assets and use it to create a reliable lifetime income stream. Yes, a pension!

You're probably wondering how your income account can grow at 7% per year guaranteed? In reality you are paying for this Longevity Insurance with the annual rider fee. But it gets even better. This income account value is growing at 7% per year *compounded*. It's often rumored that Albert Einstein once remarked that compound interest was the 8th wonder of the world. Not sure he actually said it, but regardless, compounded interest is amazing.

If done correctly, using income riders attached to these annuities can also provide you (and your spouse) an inflation adjusted income plan. Worried about losing control of your money? No need! Unlike an immediate annuity or a deferred annuity that, once annuitized is no longer your money, using these income riders doesn't mean you lose control. In fact, depending on the annuity, you have options to start and stop the flow of income, you can withdraw more money in a particular year if you need it and, upon your death, the entire remaining account balance goes to your heirs.

Why do we call this Longevity Insurance? Based on the way we structure your portfolio, we will use non-Longevity Insurance funds to provide income in the earlier years of retirement. By doing this, we can watch the income account value grow at 7% per year for a good number of years; really building up great income flows.

You may have heard of "bucket planning," where you look at your nest egg as three distinct pots of money; your NOW money, your LATER money, your NEVER money and your LEGACY money. This is part of our version, using the Longevity Insurance as part of your LATER money.

Using our proprietary program, we structure your income plan to help you keep pace with inflation, giving you a nice "pay raise" almost every year regardless of the ups and downs of the market. I call this mailbox money. Remember the way your parents' and grandparents' pensions and Social Security checks arrived in the old days?

This is income you can count on every month, and along with Social Security cost of living increases, you can sleep well at night knowing your income is secure. When we were younger, we thought that ROI was short for Return on Investment. Now that we're older (and maybe more mature) and dealing with retirement issues, we know that ROI for us means Reliability of Income.

What if you already receive enough mailbox money every month to meet your needs? Here's some great news. Since you've already got a big enough paycheck, you'll now have a *playcheck*, and every month you can decide whether to enjoy it or share it with the kids and grandkids.

Building and Maintaining a Strong Foundation
Many retirees come to realize the financial advisor that helped them accumulate money during their working years might no longer be the one to get them to the promised land of retirement income security. When you are close to retiring, you move from the accumulation stage to the protection and preservation phase. You need an expert in retirement and income planning. You need a distribution specialist, not just an accumulation specialist.

As a young kid, I remember my dad took me down to Center City (Philadelphia) one Saturday. We walked by a site where they were readying to build a skyscraper and my dad asked me what I could tell from the hole in the ground? I was totally confused. Then Dad told me the deeper the hole, the stronger the foundation and the taller the building.

Same thing with retirement planning. Think of your Social Security, pensions and income from annuities as the foundation of your house. The walls are your bank accounts, your bonds, your CDs, and your money under the mattress.

But what about that roof? What is at most risk when that tornado comes through? The roof! In retirement planning, the roof is the amount of money you have exposed to risk: stocks, mutual funds, ETFs, bond funds, REITS, UITs, Variable Annuities and commodities.

When we talked about the Rule of 100, what we were alluding to was the amount of risk in your portfolio, and yes, the size of your roof. Is your roof too big for your house? Some planners use the roof as their long term hedge against inflation. While I endorse the concept for some of your NEVER money, I believe you need to be very careful that the size of the roof is in proportion to the rest of the house.

So What's a Safe Sustainable Withdrawal Rate?
One major factor often overlooked by retirees is how much money they can safely pull out of their accounts each year without worrying about running out of money. We call this your Sustainable Withdrawal Rate and it really is the key to a successful financial retirement structure.

First, we need to measure the overall real rate of return of all your investible assets. Next, we need to know what percentage of your portfolio you plan to withdraw every year in retirement, after factoring in inflation. By feeding these two numbers into the chart, we can see whether you will run out of money and at what age.

The trick is to have a good feel for your real rate of return. Few people I've met with over the years were anywhere close in their assessment. Most had absolutely no idea. Some could tell me how well they've done in the market but they had never looked at the return on all their accounts, including non-market based accounts such as saving accounts, U.S. Savings Bonds and CDs.

Besides being safe and providing inflation adjusted income, designed to never run out as long as you (and your spouse) live, the beauty of Longevity Insurance is that it generally allows you to pull out a significantly *higher* withdrawal rate than you can comfortably pull from your other accounts.

The old rule of thumb was that with a decent portfolio, you could reasonably expect to pull out 4% per year without the worry of running out of money. Many advisors today are actually recommending 3% or less annual withdrawal, due to the long flat inflation adjusted stock market returns and very low interest rates on savings and CDs.

Knowing your SUSTAINABLE WITHDRAWAL RATE is key to not running out of money before you run out of time. Do you have an annual budget and do you stick to it? This is key to a successful retirement plan.

With 25% to 35% of your investible assets in Longevity Insurance, we can often boost the withdrawal rate to 5% or more per year and not worry about running out of income before you run out of time.

Do You Have an Inflation-Adjusted Income Plan?
This chapter has focused on income planning, taking into consideration a few key elements of retirement planning. If you've already retired and are taking Social Security, a big part of the income planning is locked in and finished.

However, regardless of whether you have already retired or hope to retire in the next five to ten years, other parts of income planning can still be modified and recalculated. Pots of money can be repositioned. Risk levels can be addressed. Tax planning strategies can still be implemented.

What we do for clients is a full-blown income plan. We look at each individual pot of money, assign a conservative rate of return, and then make calculations and decisions about when to make withdrawals from each pot, for how much and for how long. The key to our income planning success is our process of looking at the implications of each pot of money. Without this step, the results would be very unreliable.

Once your income plan is complete, you have a document you will easily understand that culminates by showing your annual inflation-adjusted income projection for each year up through 100. Sorry, but if you live to 101, you will still have a great income but you'll be on your own.

Have you done in-depth income planning? Have you factored in inflation? Has your current broker or financial planner worked with you on the distribution side? If not, find yourself an income planning specialist. If you don't know any, come see me. (I guess you knew that was coming.

CHAPTER FOUR
Social Security... Lots of Changes and None for the Better

Social Security Basics
Every election cycle, and often in-between, we hear how Social Security is going broke and how it might not be here in the future. If that's the only thing keeping you awake at night, here's some great news. Social Security isn't going anywhere anytime soon. Why? Because seniors vote, that's why! Will there be changes in ages, benefits and contribution rates in the future? You can bet on it! Will you be affected? Probably!

Maybe you've already felt the effects of the changes Congress made in October 2015. It was a beauty... with rule changes on some great benefit enhancement strategies.

Before going into all the rule changes, know this. If you're married, generally speaking, the surviving spouse will receive the higher of the two Social Security checks after the first one passes, with the smaller check going away. This alone can prove to be a big loss of income if not planned for ahead of time.

When I say "generally speaking", I am referring to some folks that never paid into Social Security or worked for the federal government or the railroads. If that's you, you are probably all too familiar with words like "offset."

Haven't retired yet? Been anxiously checking the mailbox every day waiting for your annual Social Security statement? Sad to say, but the folks at the Social Security administration now send out statements every five years, though you can keep a running track of it yourself online. So look for a paper statement shortly before you hit age 50, 55, 60 and 65 if you haven't set up an online account.

Once you get your estimate, first verify that the income history looks correct and that all years you paid into the system are recorded. Second, you might want to check out the AARP Social Security Benefits Calculator. It's pretty interesting and you can find it by visiting www.aarp.org/socialsecuritybenefits. Have fun, and when you get totally confused, come visit us and we'll help you figure it all out.

 Waiting For Your Annual Social Security Benefit Estimate?
Now you must go online to https://www.socialsecurity.gov/myaccount/

The Great Loophole Closure of 2015
If you've followed politics in the last 20 years, you know that it's rare for Congress to work together to accomplish anything. In October of 2015, however, the House, the Senate and the President all got together and agreed to... close the loopholes that allowed for some of the most popular Social Security filing strategies.

What did they close?

The first loophole they cut was the "File and Suspend" strategy. Under the previous rules, a person who had reached full retirement age could file for retired worker benefits – typically to enable a spouse to file for spousal benefits – and then suspend their own benefit. By doing so, the person would earn delayed retirement credits (up to 8% annually) and claim a higher worker benefit at a later date, up to age 70. All the while, their spouse could be receiving spousal benefits. For some couples, especially those with dual incomes, this strategy increased their total combined lifetime benefits.

Under the new rules, effective as of May 1, 2016, a worker who reaches full retirement age can still file and suspend, but their spouse can no longer collect benefits on the workers earnings record during the suspension period. This new rule effectively killed the "file and suspend" strategy for spouses. These new rules also put an end to workers requesting a retroactive lump-sum payment for the entire period their benefits were suspended.

The second loophole that the government closed was the "Restricted Application" strategy. Under the old rules, a married person who had reached full retirement age could file a "restricted application" for spousal benefits after their spouse had filed for their own worker benefits. The person collected spousal benefits while earning delayed retirement credits on their own work record. Combined with the "file and suspend" strategy, this "restricted application" strategy allowed some married couples to double dip and collect far more benefit than were intended.

The new rules close the loophole and automates a person's decision in situations like this. Now, if a person is filing for both a spousal benefit and a working benefit, they will be automatically be "deemed" to be filing for whichever single benefit is higher, and will not be able to change from one to the other in the future.

What Does The Future Hold For Social Security, And What Should You Do?

As we look at the future of Social Security (which, as I wrote earlier, I don't think is going anywhere) I suspect you will see two additional changes if you are already receiving Social Security. First, at some point in the future, they will probably tax more of your Social Security benefit than what is currently taxed. Secondly, I think you can look for the cost-of-living formula to track *price* increases and not *wage* increases. Over the long haul, economists say this will lower cost of living increases in the future.

If you're still working, you can expect changes to Social Security as well. Full retirement age (FRA in Social Security parlance) begins to climb from 66 to 67 for those born after 1960. Look for Congress to again pass new legislation to raise FRA past age 67 as our longevity increases. And, right now, they stop taking Social Security taxes out of your paycheck once you hit $127,200. Look for that number to increase in the coming years.

For those who paid in maximum taxes over the years, if you are 66 this year your gross monthly benefit would be $2,687. Should you start collecting before FRA, any earnings over $16,920 per year will cause you to lose $1.00 in benefits for every $2.00 you earn over the $16,920. In your 66th year you can earn $44,880 without losing any of your benefit. Nothing complicated here...right? Don't we just love the Social Security rules?

In closing out, there are a lot of takeaways in this chapter and, regardless of how changes apply or will apply to you, it's important to you (and your spouse if married) that you sit down with a Social Security agent far in advance of your retirement date to better understand benefit options and implications. I have found the staff at Social Security to be amongst the finest in the federal bureaucracy.

Since I often accompany my clients to the Social Security office, I can tell you first hand that they are generally great to work with.

And after all this... you will still love Social Security... if not Congress. You just maybe don't love it as much as you did before you read this chapter.

CHAPTER FIVE
Individual Retirement Accounts, or Not?
Why Your IRA Is Really an Internal Revenue Account

Nothing confounds retirees more than all the confusing rules concerning their IRAs (Individual Retirement Accounts), 401(k)s, 403(b)s and deferred compensation plans. In the financial planning world, all these accounts are called Qualified Accounts. What qualifies them as Qualified Accounts? Thought you'd never ask.

Except for Roth IRAs and Roth 401(k)s, none of this money has ever been taxed. So, every time you take a distribution, every time you pull out money, along with the withdrawal comes a tax bill from your favorite uncle. Hence the nickname Internal Revenue Account!

IRS Publication 590 (IRS.gov under Forms and Publications) is around 110 pages long. Literally hundreds of books have been written trying to properly interpret these 110 pages. Go figure! Probably the two best known authorities on IRAs are Ed Slott and Natalie Choate. Most of what I've learned over the years came from these two people.

Surely, I can't do justice to all the complicated rules surrounding IRAs. However, in the next few pages, I will provide about 95% of what the average retiree needs to know about their IRA and the Internal Revenue Service.

Until What Age Can I Add to my IRA?
Starting in the year you turn 70 ½, you are forbidden to contribute to a traditional IRA. Up until this age, if you or your spouse has sufficient

income, you can contribute to your IRA.

So When Must I Take That Initial RMD?
IRA holders have to begin taking minimum distributions from their accounts by April 1 of the year following the year they turn 70½ years old. To figure out the amount you're required to withdraw for the first year, you would divide the value of your traditional IRA as of Dec. 31 of the previous year by the life-expectancy factor for your age. You can find the appropriate life-expectancy factor in IRS Publication 590 at irs.gov under "Forms and Publications."

For example, if you turned 70 on May 1, 2017, you'll be 70½ on Nov. 1, 2017. So you'd be required to take your first distribution by April 1, 2018. You'd have to take your second distribution by Dec. 31, 2018. So in this situation you'd be taking two distributions in one year, which could put you into a higher tax bracket. In this example, many folks would begin taking distributions in 2017 if taking two distributions in 2018 pushes you into the next marginal tax bracket.

Most people use the "Uniform Lifetime" table. For that first year, you would look up the life-expectancy factor for age 70 if your birthday is between Jan. 1 and June 30; use the factor for 71 if your birthday is between July 1 and Dec. 31.

Spouse 10 Years Younger?
When your spouse is your IRA beneficiary and is more than 10 years younger than you, the IRS lets you use a distribution schedule that allows you to take smaller required distributions. The idea is that they are trying to ensure that there is enough income left for the second to die due to the big age discrepancy. Isn't the IRS really sweet? But seriously, this is a good thing since it saves you taxes if you don't need the distribution.

The life expectancy used while the owner is alive is the joint life expectancy of the owner and spouse, recalculated each year. When the owner dies, the exception no longer applies.

The new lower RMD amounts are based on an IRS table that assumes, for calculation purposes, that your beneficiary is 10 years younger than you. If your spouse is your sole beneficiary and is more than 10 years your junior, you can use your spouse's actual age instead, producing an even lower RMD.

Do You Have an Inherited IRA?

Did you receive an IRA as an inheritance? If so, and if you were a non-spousal beneficiary, you must begin taking distributions the year after the year of death of the IRA benefactor. This applies to traditional and Roth IRAs, along with 401(k)s, 403(b)s and deferred comp plans.

Since it is an inherited IRA, you must use a different table to calculate your annual distribution. Bottom line, your friends at the IRS make you take a bigger percentage distribution each year than the benefactor needed to take based on age. This way the IRS gets you to pay more taxes than you otherwise would need to.

See, I told you. The folks at the IRS love you and they love your _Internal Revenue Accounts!_

Have a 401(k) with Highly Appreciated Company Stock?

Stop! Before you roll over this 401(k) account with highly appreciated company stock to an IRA, you need to talk with an IRA expert. Using a little known regulation in the tax code, you could save thousands and thousands of dollars in future taxes on this company stock. This strategy doesn't apply to mutual funds or the stable value fund in your 401(k). Just your company stock in your 401(k) and only if it's really gone up in price over the years.

401(k) Contributions After Age 70 ½

First, we always recommend you move your 401(k) to an IRA once you leave your employer, whether just changing jobs or retiring. On occasion, there might be a good reason to leave the money with your employer, but I rarely see situations where this makes sense.

In the case of a 401(k), as long as you are employed by the firm where you have the 401(k), you can continue to make contributions past age 70 ½. In addition, if over 70 ½, you need not start taking RMDs from just this one 401(k) until the year after you retire. However, you will need to take RMDs from all other IRAs and 401(k)s once you turn 70 ½.

Underestimate and Face a 50% Penalty
The folks at IRS are very understanding. They bend over backwards to help you, except if you don't follow the tax laws or don't pay your taxes. Otherwise, they are great people.

They are so kind that, should you not take the proper annual RMD, they will only fine you a 50% penalty on the shortfall. Hey, it could be 75%.

For example, let's say you were required to take out $10,000 last year but you only took a $6,000 distribution. The shortfall of $4,000 would result in a $2,000 penalty (50%) plus interest.

See, I told you. The folks at the IRS do have a heart!

Can You Avoid Paying Taxes on Your IRA?
Like many of you, I get invitations in the mail all the time for financial seminar dinners. Some weeks I could eat out almost every night on a broker or insurance agent's dime.

I love reading the bullet points on the invitations. Whoever writes these invitations should win a literary award for being the most creative and deceptive. Nevertheless, it's fun reading.

The best bullet point says that you can avoid paying taxes on your IRA. What they forget to tell you is that for this to happen, you will need to convert all your Qualified Accounts to Roth IRAs and pay a big tax bill up front.

We'll talk more about Roth conversions in the next chapter. For now, just know that at age 70 ½ you must begin taking distributions and paying the tax on traditional accounts, but NOT on your Roths.

Are You Upside Down?
Not literally, but in your portfolio? Let me explain. The majority of the portfolios I review have the bulk of their risk in their qualified accounts including IRAs, 401(k)s and 403(b) accounts, and less or often very little risk in their non-qualified or non-IRA accounts.

Why is there often more risk in your qualified accounts such as IRAs? Usually a big chunk of IRA money came from either 401(k) rollovers or 403(b) rollovers from tax sheltered annuities. How was the bulk of this money often invested? In mutual stock and bond funds and perhaps some company stock.

Often retirees just roll these accounts over and leave the funds pretty much intact with the same custodian that manages the 401(k) or 403(b), and keep them still mostly in mutual funds.

At the same time, I see lots of CDs, individual bonds and money market funds in non-IRA accounts, along with some stocks and mutual funds.

As a tax planning strategy, this is often not the best approach as you can't fully take advantage of some tax breaks. Why do I say this? Think about it: you pay ordinary income tax rates on your IRA distributions and capital gains rates on your non-IRA gains.

Most of my retired clients are in the 25% or 28% tax bracket, and that's the tax they are paying on their IRA distributions. But what are capital gains rates? Right now, the rate is 15% for most folks, and if you're a high earner in the 39.6% bracket, your rate is only 20%. Still better than 25% or 28%.

A Smart Tax Planning Strategy

For many retirees, the smart move is to have more of their risk outside their IRA accounts, and more safe money in the IRAs. You can't take advantage of market losses in an IRA. You just pay taxes on the required distribution, regardless of how the investments are performing.

IRAs are designed to give you a predictable income stream during retirement. What happens when the market tanks 20% or 30% or even 40%? You still must take a distribution based on your IRA totals from the last day of last year. You will be pulling out a pretty hefty chunk of the current lower IRA value. Worse than that, you still pay the full tax bill on the distribution based on ordinary income tax rates.

You have no way of taking advantage of capital gains tax laws, where you can offset gains with losses. Have a huge gain in a stock and want to sell it but don't want to pay a huge tax bill? Go through your portfolio of non-IRA holdings, see where you have losses, and sell them off also. This way you are balancing out your gains and losses, and paying less or no taxes. If you do owe taxes, it's at the 15% capital gains rate.

Remember we talked about Longevity Insurance in the last chapter? Why not lower your risk in your IRAs, use a portion to buy Longevity Insurance and move more risk to your non-IRA accounts? This way you have the best of both worlds.

This ties in perfectly with our bucket planning where we use the IRA money in bucket two to create pension money you can't outlive. Bucket one is what we refer to as NOW money, bucket two as LATER money and bucket three we call NEVER money. We generally can use bucket three for long term risk such as mutual funds and stocks where we have a long time horizon (good lord willing).

IRAs and Medicaid Planning

One last planning tool you should know about concerns how IRAs function in Medicaid planning. The subject of Medicaid is discussed in more detail in Chapter Nine, but since this is a potentially important piece of information, and since you may never make it to the back of the book, I thought I'd sneak this in now.

If you are married and your spouse needs to go into a nursing home, in Pennsylvania, your IRA is not subject to spend-down. This book was mainly written for folks in my state, and I am not familiar with the rules in all 50 states. If you are a resident of another state, please check with a specialist in this area.

 In Pennsylvania, if your spouse is confined to a nursing home, YOUR IRA is not subject to spend-down to care for your spouse. It's very important to check the rules in your state.

We refer to the spouse who needs the care as the *nursing home spouse* and the stay at home spouse as the *community spouse*. In Pennsylvania, IRAs and other qualified accounts of the community spouse are not subject to spend-down for the care of the nursing home spouse.

Generally, my advice to my clients is that if one needs to go into a nursing home, it should be the one with the smaller IRA. How's that for logic? Better yet, why not both of you live well into your 90s and die in your sleep, at home together?

Still Confused?

As I said at the beginning of this chapter, IRAs are very confusing. We've just scratched the surface here but we tried to cover those questions most often asked by my clients. One of the most popular Lunch & Learn events we do on a regular basis is on different parts of IRA planning. To get on our mailing list for all our education events, you can go to our website at www.franklinrs.com or call us at 215-657-9200.

CHAPTER SIX
The Conversion Dilemma: To Roth or Not to Roth?

One of the most frequent questions I'm asked at an initial consultation is whether folks should convert their IRAs to Roth IRAs. At the end of the day, the majority of my middle income clients decide not to convert additional funds to a Roth, or they decide to perhaps gradually convert a small portion to Roth.

One reason to seriously consider conversions is tax rates: Ed Slott, renowned IRA guru, always pounds the podium, raises his voice and yells "taxes are on sale!"

What does he mean? Projections for the federal budget going forward are bleak. Blame it on the baby boomers because our Social Security and Medicare are budget busters. Add in Medicaid and it's easy to see how the deficit will keep climbing.

No need to opine over how we got into this mess. It's been building for many years and won't be solved quickly. However, with the government borrowing over 30 cents of every dollar it spends, we know something has to give. And while I'm no rocket scientist, nor an economist with a PhD, even a knucklehead like me realizes there are only two ways to cut the deficit: tax increases and spending cuts.

Both will be needed in the years ahead to get our fiscal house in order before this runaway train crashes and China whips our behind.

Even if we cut spending, eventually tax rates will need to increase, and not just on the rich, since the revenue that would be generated from taxing the millionaires and billionaires won't begin to fix the problem.

Since we focus our practice on middle income folks, quite often I have the pleasure of telling my clients that when we add up all their accounts and the net value of their homes, they are in fact millionaires. The typical reaction is for them to laugh. Being a millionaire today isn't the same as being one 20 or 30 years ago, due to our old friend called "inflation." Reminds me of one of my favorite humorists, Yogi Berra, when he said, "the future ain't what it used to be."

To illustrate the point, let's assume you have a million dollar pot of investible assets at the time you retire. Taking an often-recommended 4% income from your nest egg, known as a sustainable withdrawal rate, yields you only $40,000 per year before taxes. I can tell you that most folks are horrified when they realize that the million bucks they saved doesn't really go too far today.

So, what's all this have to do with Roth conversions? If taxes are eventually going to rise, now might be a good time to convert some or all of your IRAs, 401(k)s and 403(b)s to Roth IRAs. But what are the factors one should take into consideration, other than future potential tax rates? There are quite a few.

Reasons to Consider Conversions:
- If your income tax bracket will be higher in retirement, you are a potential candidate for conversion. Folks that retire in their 60s often live off their non-IRA accounts and maybe their pensions until they turn 70 ½, when they must begin taking their RMDs. At the same time, some of these retirees also hold off on Social Security until age 70.

  What they fail to realize is that when they start taking their RMDs and Social Security, their income will rise drastically. If this is your future scenario, converting some or all of your IRAs may make sense.

- If you have the ability to report lower income in any given year, converting in that year could lower your income tax on the conversion. Again, this is often the case in the early years of retirement, before taking Social Security and RMDs. I often see folks with pretty low income in their 60s, a perfect time to consider converting.
- Do you or will you need the IRA required minimum distributions to live on once you hit 70 ½? If not, you may be a great candidate for a Roth conversion. I have clients where both husband and wife were school teachers and get big pensions and big Social Security checks. Being conservative, they don't even touch the wife's pension and they live very nicely. No more need to reuse the tea bag – or to cut coupons, for that matter. After teaching kids and dealing with parents for 40 years, trust me, they deserve it.

  As they inch closer to that magic 70 ½, their big question is, why do they need to take the distribution since they don't need the money? Remember, I called your IRA an Internal Revenue Account. This is why. The IRS demands you take your RMDs starting at 70 ½ so they get the tax revenue. You must withdraw the money, pay the taxes and then you can move it to a non-IRA account. Then you can save it, spend it or gift it.
- If it's your desire that your beneficiaries receive an income tax-free inheritance, a Roth conversion may be right for you. A few of my clients have an overriding desire to leave their kids and grandkids in the best possible shape. I've seen where folks deny themselves the small luxuries of life because they want to leave more to their kids or grandkids.

  Listen, I love my kids dearly. And all other things being equal, I'll leave them a nice inheritance. But while I'm still around, I want to enjoy my money and my life.

There are folks I run into on both sides of the spectrum. There are the retirees I just mentioned who don't want to spend a dime, so more goes to the kids. Then there are the ones with those bumper stickers. You've seen them: *I'm Spending My Kids' Inheritance* slapped on the back bumper. They're the same folks who tell me they plan to run out of money the same time they run out of time. Better yet, they tell me their goal is to have the check to the funeral home bounce!

Reasons NOT to Consider Conversions:

- If you will need your RMDs to live on in retirement, you may not be a great candidate. For some folks, paying the tax bill every year vs. a big lump sum check to your favorite Uncle Sam makes more sense.
- Do you expect to be in a lower tax bracket in retirement? Let's say you are still working and earning a big salary, putting you into a high tax bracket. You worked the numbers and figure you'll be in a lower tax bracket when you retire. For you, a conversion may not make sense.
- If you have an aversion to paying the income tax up front and do not trust the government to keep the tax-free deal, maybe conversion isn't for you. I've had clients who just about passed out in my conference room when they realized how much the conversion would cost.

  One client said to me, after he came to, that he loves his country very much. Considers himself a patriot. But when faced with the thought of writing out a check to his favorite uncle, he said there was just no way he could get his hand to cooperate so he could write out a check to the IRS for $140,000.
- If you do not have the liquidity to pay the tax on the conversion from non-retirement assets, maybe a conversion isn't for you. What am I talking about? Some folks think they can pull out the IRA money for a Roth conversion and use that money to pay the

taxes on the conversion. Good try, but it doesn't work that way.

You must rollover every dime you convert. You can't use any of it to pay the tax on the conversion. So, where do you get the money to pay the taxes? Not from your IRA. That would result in double taxation, since the additional money you'd pull from the IRA to pay the Roth conversion tax would also be taxed. So, you'd need to pull out even more from your IRA to cover the taxes on the money you pulled out to pay the tax. Confused? You're not alone.

- If you have named a charity, church or school, which are exempt from income tax, as the beneficiary of the IRA, why convert that portion? There will be no taxes due upon your death for the IRA money that goes to a non-profit. Why pay the conversion tax?

As an aside, a good tax strategy when leaving money to churches or charity is to leave them the IRA money, and leave your heirs your non-IRA money. This makes sense, since there may be a very low, or even no, tax bill attached to that part of the inheritance being left to your heirs, due to what's known as the "step up in basis." Talk to your CPA for tax advice or come visit with me.

Still Working Past Age 70 ½?
With an IRA, you can't continue adding to your account after you hit age 70, even if you are still working. Not so with a Roth. As long as you have earned income you can continue to feed your Roth with new contributions, up to the IRS approved annual limits.

Does this make sense? For many people it does. If you or your spouse are working, you can each put up to $6,500 per year into your Roth for a total of $13,000 per year. The only catch is that, between the two of you, there must be a combined total earned income of $13,000 per year. So basically, you can put all your earned income into Roths if you are earning less than, or up to $13,000 annually. Note, there are upper income limitations as well. Check with your CPA.

What If You Are Younger? Should You Feed Your Roth?
Definitely! Remember, the Roth IRA didn't become law until 1998. By then, most baby boomers or pre-boomers had amassed much of their 401(k) money, taking the annual tax deductions for their contributions. Few were able to move their money to IRAs while working and companies didn't offer Roth 401(k)s.

Today, all that is changing. Many 401(k)s allow for you to choose between traditional pre-tax contributions and a Roth post-tax contribution. What should you do? My recommendation is to forego the tax deduction now and feed your money into Roth accounts, if your employer gives you the option. You'll thank me years from now when you realize there is no huge tax bill attached to your retirement accounts, what Ed Slott refers to as the "Ticking IRA Tax Time Bomb" as discussed in his 2003 book, *The Retirement Savings Time Bomb...and How to Defuse It*.

Over the next twenty to thirty years, your retirement accounts will now grow tax-free vs. tax deferred. And what's on sale now? Taxes!

Should I Do Partial Roth Conversions?
Great question, and like most great questions, it all depends. How's that for a definitive answer? Maybe I should have been a politician instead of a retirement planner?

I often recommend that people convert their retirement accounts incrementally to Roths, a little bit each year. How much? Lots of times, it's based on the tax bracket you are in, and how much room you have to convert, before it pushes you into the next tax bracket.

Let's say you and your spouse are in the 15% tax bracket, which goes up to $75,900 in income. This year, your combined income is only $40,000. I might recommend converting up to $35,900 this year to a Roth, keeping you in the 15% tax bracket. See? It's not so difficult as long as you have a pretty good idea what your income will be for the year. That's where the financial planners and CPAs come in.

Suppose I Want to Leave My Kids in Great Shape but...
I hear this often. The "but" is, "But I can't stomach the idea of writing out that big check to the IRS. Do you have any ideas, Peter?" A matter of fact, I do. You'll read all about it in the next chapter when I discuss the dreaded product called life insurance. Stay tuned!

CHAPTER SEVEN
Is Life Insurance Really a Dirty Word, or Two?

Folks come into my office all the time and tell me the two "products" they hate most are annuities and life insurance. As a full-service retirement planner dually licensed in life and health insurance, as well as a Registered Investment Advisor, we can handle all of your investment, insurance, tax and income planning, as well as set you up with an estate plan crafted to you and your family's customized needs. These are important puzzle pieces and they all need to fit together.

I try to tell folks not to jump to conclusions, but 98% of the time, they already have. Needless to say, you must have some pretty compelling reasons for people to change their minds. In fact, I never ask people to change. As Will Rogers said many years ago, "The only person that likes change is a baby with a wet diaper."

Instead, I ask people to make new decisions based on new information. People usually chuckle, give me a strange look and sit back, cross their arms and say something like "Ok, prove it to me."

Now, where were we? Almost forgot, life insurance. Bottom line, life insurance is really nothing more than a tax elimination and wealth transfer tool. Where else can you get totally legitimate, tax-free money today?

My goal in this chapter is to give you new information about the beauty of life insurance and the many solutions it can provide in retirement and estate planning.

The big thing to remember with all life insurance, other than term life, is that you are not throwing money into a black hole. Far from that, life insurance can be a savings and investment plan. The returns on your investment can be pretty amazing, depending on how soon you die. (Oops, there I go. I promised Jeremy I'd leave out my sick humor in my chapters. Hope he doesn't kill me when he reads this.)

Can You Get Underwritten?
For some of you, this will be a very short chapter, as you may decide to stop reading in a minute or two. Oh, not because you're not enjoying the book, and not because you're not getting lots of useful information in the book, but rather, because you'll realize you're just not a candidate for life insurance. If that's the case, skip to the next chapter. I won't tell anybody. While the biggest growth today in the life insurance market is with retired people, the most difficult part is often qualifying or getting underwritten. Bottom line is that if you're in bad health, the insurance company will pass on the opportunity to underwrite a policy. It's not that they don't like you. It's just that they hate paying claims and only want to insure folks that have a low risk of checking out anytime soon. Now you know why the life insurance companies have all the money.

All that being said, the life insurance industry is much more lenient on whom they will insure today when compared to the old days. With all the advances in health care and with people living longer on average, life insurers today are writing cases that they'd never have written ten or fifteen years ago.

In addition, many insurers now use what is called *table shaving*. If you are not in the best of health, but still insurable, you will be rated and up-charged for the policy. Instead of being rated *preferred* or *standard*, you might be rated a *table 3* or *table 4*. Not so good in the insurer's eyes, but still healthy enough to buy green bananas.

So what are some insurers doing? To keep the premiums attractive, they do this *table shaving* thing, where they will improve your rating and allow you to purchase the policy, as if you are a standard risk.

By now you're saying to yourself, "Okay, Peter, what's the bottom line with this underwriting stuff?" Easy: unless you are in really bad health, we'll try to see if we can get you underwritten so you can take advantage of all the great tools available by incorporating life insurance into your retirement, tax elimination and estate plan. Let's look at some of these planning techniques.

Not Yet Retired and Not Sure About Your Pension Survivor Benefit?
It's almost that time. You've clocked your years and are just itching for that gold watch. There are trepidations. I hear the wife often tell me that she took her husband for better or for worse, but not for his being home for lunch every day.

So many decisions to make. When to take Social Security? If married, when should my spouse take his or hers? How are we going to cover the health insurance until we both turn 65 and go on Medicare? If you're younger, a better question may be whether there will still be Medicare by the time you retire, but "that's a whole 'nother talk show."

If you are lucky enough to retire with a pension and you are married, decisions need to be made about whether to take a smaller monthly payment with a survivor benefit and, if so, how much? Many companies will allow you to take the highest pension payment with no survivor benefit and a smaller monthly pension with a 50% or 100% survivor benefit. The federal government usually offers a 55% survivor benefit. With state workers and school teachers in my home state of Pennsylvania, there are additional options, as you can assign the survivor benefit to non-spousal beneficiaries, such as your kids.

By now you're wondering, what does all this have to do with life insurance? I thought you'd never ask. One successful strategy we employ is for the spouse to take their maximum monthly pension and no survivor benefit. We then take the difference between the maximum payout and the minimum payout (with the 100% survivor benefit), and see how much life insurance we can buy with this money.

For example, you're about to retire and would receive $5,000 per month (isn't that nice?), with no survivor benefit and $4,000 per month (still not too shabby!), with a 100% survivor benefit. What we do at this point is to see how much life insurance we can buy on you for $1,000 per month premium. Once we have those numbers, we can make some very important decisions.

Part of the calculus is longevity. Trust me, if you could only tell me how long you'll live, it would make my job so much easier. But of course, none of us know that.

If it's your pension and you are taking the max with no survivor benefit, but you also bought life insurance, it will be easier to manage your income, should your spouse predecease you. Yes, you'll lose the smaller of the two Social Security checks, but the pension would be higher, because you did take the maximum pension payout.

Now, you'd need to make a decision on the life insurance policy you purchased, in case your spouse dies first. You could either keep it and change the beneficiaries to your kids, grandkids, nieces or nephews, or you could cancel the policy and save yourself that $1,000 per month you were paying for the policy.

Now let's flip the scenario. You took your pension with no survivor benefit and you die – prematurely, of course. Did you protect your spouse and their future income? If you bought life insurance, it would pay off and we would invest it to provide pension replacement income. What if you didn't buy life insurance for your spouse? That's what we call "moving to a new neighborhood." Oh...and it's generally not a better neighborhood.

Remember what we talked about before? You need a retirement planning expert to help you navigate retirement, not an accumulation expert like your old broker. And by the way, why are they called brokers? Some say because the longer you work with them, the broker you get!

To Roth or Not to Roth? Again?

Calm down and give me a minute to explain. You are correct; the last chapter was devoted to Roth conversions. But suppose you just can't write out that big check to Uncle Sam. Now what? Bet you can't guess? Life insurance. Once again, you are correct!

 Before you convert your IRA to a tax-free ROTH, consider the leverage afforded instead with tax-free Life Insurance. Have your financial planner run some illustrations first!

Let's take a look at a hypothetical case:

We'll call him Bob. Bob wanted to discuss converting his IRAs to Roths. I told him he had come to the right place. We went through all the decision-making steps discussed in the last chapter, and Bob was a perfect candidate. Just one small, little problem: he couldn't write the check. We were looking at a $400,000 IRA and his initial thought was to convert it all. He and his wife were in the 35% tax bracket, which meant it would have cost Bob about $140,000 to do the conversion. Ouch.

Since he didn't need his RMDs, I showed Bob how he could use the RMDs to buy life insurance, and laid out the short term and long term benefits of this strategy. At 70 ½, Bob would have needed to pull out approximately $15,000 per year and pay taxes on that money, so we used this as a beginning point. In his case, this would net up to around $12,000 per year, once he and his wife retired, which would be very soon.

Bob then gave me permission to run quotes for $15,000 per year in premium, figuring he'd use other money to pay the taxes. By this time, Bob was all revved up about the leveraging effect of life insurance. We ran quotes for Bob and were able to get him a universal life policy with a death benefit of around $600,000. Bob decided to apply for the coverage and was underwritten.

So what happened? Instead of writing out a big, fat check to his favorite "Uncle," Bob instead signed up to pay an annual premium of $15,000. Had he done the conversion, his estate would have been diminished by $140,000. By going the insurance route, his portfolio was only down by $15,000. Bob thought that was a much better idea.

If, God forbid, Bob dies prematurely, his estate would be in much better shape. Let's say Bob had $1 million in investable assets when he first came to visit with me. Had he done the Roth conversion, he'd now have an estate valued at $860,000 after paying the $140,000 in taxes.

Using the life insurance method, Bob's estate would now include $985,000 (since he used $15,000 for the first year's premium) and $600,000 in tax-free life insurance, for a total estate value of $1,585,000. No doubt Bob would be sorely missed by his wife and kids, but they sure would have a newfound respect for his investing and estate planning acumen. They'd throw one heck of a celebration of life party, using his money, of course, to pay for the bash.

So let's look at this. Which number, $840,000 or $1,585,000, do you like better? What if Bob dies two years into the policy? Which number, $870,000 (figure some growth) or $1,600,000 (again, figure some growth) do you like better?

The beauty is that this strategy has about a 20-25 year break-even point, with an internal rate of return after all those years of over 4%.

Not a bad long-term investment, and a safe one at that. Of course, if you are looking for the best possible investment return, all you need do is die shortly after the policy is issued. Wait till you see that rate of return on your investment. Too bad you won't be around to crow to your friends about your foresight. (This example is for illustrative purposes only and is not intended to project the performance of a specific investment and is based on the financial strength of the insuring company and that certain terms and limitations may apply.)

It's All About Tax Elimination and Wealth Transfer
Once senior citizens (or what I like to call, Seasoned Citizens) really understand the power of life insurance, they often look at the planning techniques with much more interest.

How else are we using life insurance in today's retirement and estate plans? Thought you'd never ask. Let me run through a few concepts that folks use to leverage their money.

"Second to Die" policies are often used to transfer wealth, and are underwritten on both husband and wife. The premiums are lower than on a single life, since it doesn't pay off until the second of you die. Go figure!

Usually these second-to-die policies are wrapped up in an ILIT, short for Irrevocable Life Insurance Trust. The beauty is that the death benefit will go to the heirs with no estate taxes.

While you are living, we use life insurance to leverage the money you may have sitting in non-IRA annuities. Most people never touch these annuities, and when they or their heirs do take distributions, the gains must be withdrawn before the principal, and these gains are taxed as ordinary income.

What we often do is use the 10% penalty-free withdrawals, allowed in most annuities, to fund a life insurance policy for the kids or grandkids.

Not only are you leveraging an asset you might never touch, but also more than offsetting the tax consequences of these annuities for your heirs, as the tax on the gains don't go away after you take that last limo ride.

Often parents realize there could be a huge tax attached to their IRAs if their heirs decide to cash them in for whatever reason. This really haunts many of my conservative clients: the thought that the money they have worked a lifetime to accumulate will be spent before they're even buried. With proper estate planning, much of that may be avoidable. Oops, I digressed again.

Folks often use life insurance to pay all the estate and inheritance taxes, and still have enough money to pay the taxes on the IRAs. Your kids will be so happy. Take my word for it, since you won't be here. Another great planning tool!

Have Old Life Insurance Policies?
Another great way to leverage your money is to do a quick analysis of any old life insurance policies you own. We often see cash value built up in these policies but the death benefit is still the same as it was many moons ago.

We've been very successful in rolling over this cash value into new policies with higher death benefits. Sounds crazy, you're thinking, since the policy owner is now much older. True! But over the past 30 years the rates on life insurance have come down drastically as we live longer.

You should contact your life insurance company and request an "in-force illustration," to see how the policy is performing and what actuarial tables were used on your old policies.

One Last Idea for You Young Ones
For the most part, the life insurance strategies we have discussed so far work best for those over age 60. But what if you are 45 or 50 and have

term policies in place to handle the lost income and kids' education if you check out early? We have a strategy for you, also known as "Be Your Own Banker."

Using this concept allows you to build up cash value rapidly and take loans from your policy at a very low interest rate. Basically, it's a way for you to be your own banker using that often hated, and seldom respected tool, called life insurance.

Time to Wrap it Up
We devoted this entire chapter to life insurance because it is such an amazing planning tool. Sure, it's boring and vanilla compared to other investment schemes. Not sexy at all. But think about it: in good times and bad, life insurance is a steady strategy that always pays off.

More and more, Jeremy and I use these life insurance strategies to solve a myriad of estate planning problems and to create plans that really leverage all the fine work you did in saving and building your nest egg.

When folks go through our Four Step Discovery Review Process, it will become pretty clear whether any of these tools might make sense for their estate plan. The most important piece is to not procrastinate. Schedule some time now to visit, and let's see how we can enhance your estate plan, using life insurance for tax elimination and wealth transfer.

FOUR STEP DISCOVERY REVIEW PROCESS	
Income Planning	*Tax Planning*
Risk Exposure/Risk Comfort Level	*Estate & Legacy Planning*

CHAPTER EIGHT
Gift Now or Make Them Wait?

One of the biggest dilemmas faced by some of our clients is whether to gift to kids or grandkids now, or make them wait until after they're gone. With continuing economic challenges, including the skyrocketing national debt and unemployment statistics, many retirees continue to share with us their concerns about the younger generations.

When it comes to tax implications of gifts, there are two types of gifts you can make without penalty. The annual exclusion gift, which more people are familiar with, allows you to give to any and every person you wish, up to $14,000 per year with no paperwork, no tax implications and no other ramifications.

For example, let's say you are married, have two married children and four grandchildren. You and your spouse can gift to all these family members each year, including your favorite son-in-law or daughter-in-law. Isn't that exciting? So for this family, Mom and Dad could each gift a total of $112,000, or a total of $224,000 for the couple, and the only thing they need do is write out the checks. Best thing is, you can do this every year until you go broke.

Five Million Dollar Lifetime Gift Exemption
The second type of taxable gift is the lifetime exemption gift. In addition to the $14,000 you can gift every year to anybody you want, there is also a lifetime gift exemption. As of April 2017, you can gift up to $5.49 million over your lifetime with no tax ramifications and just a little paperwork. Remember, if you gift someone $14,000 this year, there's

no paperwork. Gift that same person $14,001 and you need to let your favorite "uncle" know by filling out form 709 when doing your year-end taxes. When you exceed the $14,000 limit in any one year for any gift recipient, you need to do the 709, but no taxes due from the one that gifted or the one that received the gift.

Nothing is ever as easy as it sounds, but this really is, unless you wind up in a nursing home in the next five years. More on that in the next chapter.

Two final notes on the estate and gift tax. First, this exemption is now indexed for inflation as calculated by the government. Second, if your $5.49 million is burning a hole in your pocket and you decide to gift to the kids, albeit begrudgingly, know that Congress could always decide to change this hefty exemption. Remember, the only thing certain in life is taxes and death...not Congress.

Will Your Kids Have Pensions?
I often hear from my clients how concerned they are that their kids are not doing as well as they did. They often cite how expensive it is to raise a family today, and how difficult it is for their kids to sock away very much for the future. They often worry even more about their grandchildren.

On top of that, I so often hear my clients talk about Social Security and Medicare, wondering if it will still be around by the time their kids retire. They wonder out loud what will become of the younger generation, and they are extremely concerned about the future of our country.

Often parents tell me that one or two kids are doing great and that another one or two aren't. Sometimes, I see the pain written all over their faces. These folks want to go to their grave knowing their kids are going to be ok.

One technique often used is to buy a life insurance policy in your son's or daughter's name. The technique we use is to fund a life policy, so that it can be used in the future as a "tax-free bank." You're probably asking, what is a tax-free bank? Be patient. I'm getting to it.

For example, let's say you have a 35-year-old daughter. She's married, has a few kids and works really hard to make ends meet. She just can't seem to save much. You could gift her $10,000 a year for 20 years which would fund the life insurance policy.

Here are the details of this example:
- Issue Age: 36
- # of years for full funding: 20 years
- Pension Payout: At age 65, this policy can pay out $68,000 per year for the next 25 years or until age 90, tax-free!

Sure, it's life insurance, and yes, there is a death benefit. In this example, the death benefit is slightly over $900,000. If your child is raising a family, this policy could be a god-send if needed. But should your child live a long life, switching the life insurance policy automatically into a tax-free pension will sure come in handy.

This gifting program works for kids, grandkids, nieces and nephews. We coordinate all the details and make sure the beneficiaries are set up the way you want. We will also handle the gift tax schedule for the IRS if needed.

Talk about giving a gift that keeps on giving, this is the ultimate. Gift now and secure your kids' future and their families' future. In Chapter 11, we'll discuss more about gifting to the grandchildren and how to protect your gift for years to come.

One last thing, the dreaded Five-Year Look Back. Unfortunately, the IRS and the folks over at Medicaid never coordinated this whole gifting thing, should you wind up in a nursing home. More on that in the next chapter.

Gifting Strategies with Trusts
There aren't too many people that like the idea of giving their kids or grandkids large gifts with no strings attached. There are two problems with doing so. When you make a large gift, you have absolutely no control over what happens to those assets. Second, if you need long-term care before five years pass from that gift, you could be disqualified and penalized from Medicaid for months or years!

Using a special trust to hold large gifts can solve that problem and provide both you and your heirs great benefits. We can use this trust as a strategy for long term care costs, shrinking our estate for federal estate tax purposes (not many people are affected by the federal estate tax right now), and finally, it can be used as a strategy to help your kids, while protecting them from themselves and others.

 This special trust is called an Irrevocable Trust and is referred to as a Grantors Trust, Income Only Trust, Medicaid Income Only Trust, and assorted other names.

Although there are many fancy names for this type of trust, here's what you really need to know about a trust like this:
1. **IRREVOCABLE**: If a trust is irrevocable, you as the grantor of the trust cannot change the terms of the trust, nor can you terminate it. Therefore, an irrevocable trust must be carefully designed to think ahead. The reason we make the trust irrevocable is so that the assets within it are no longer in your name. That's important if you're trying to shrink your estate for long-term care planning or federal estate tax planning.
2. **GRANTORS**: If the trust is a Grantors trust, you, as the grantor, still pay income Taxes on the trust while you're living, and your heirs get the benefits tax-free.
3. **INCOME ONLY**: Even though you give up control over the trust and the assets within it, you can establish the trust in such a way that allows you to receive the income from any trust assets,

60

while preserving the principal for your heirs. This strategy still keeps the trust assets out of your name and out of your estate, even though you have rights to the income.

Irrevocable trusts combined with gifting can work wonders. It is difficult for many people to part with their money, so this strategy can appear risky. This strategy shouldn't be used haphazardly. Rather, it should be part of a careful plan with full analysis. Perhaps you only put 20% of your estate in an irrevocable trust, because you know you will never use that 20%. You can shelter those assets from long-term care costs and make a structured gift to your kids.

Speaking of long-term care costs, they are discussed more in Chapter 8. As discussed in that chapter, there is a five-year look back period for any gifts. What that means is before you can go on Medicaid, the government will look to see if you made any gifts in the last five years, and if you have, that will delay when you can qualify for Medicaid benefits. Irrevocable trusts can be great tools to plan well in advance of needing long-term care. But it's never a perfect science. Who knows when and if you'll need to go into a nursing home? The beauty of an irrevocable trust is that if set up correctly the principal would still be preserved in the trust; and the trustee could have the discretion to transfer those assets back to you if needed.

As you have read, irrevocable trusts and gifting can make a lot of sense for some people, but it can get complicated. Your situation, circumstances, goals and health need to be taken into account when doing this type of planning. There is no *one-size-fits-all* solution. In the next chapter, you'll learn more about long-term care costs and additional strategies for dealing with those costs.

CHAPTER NINE
What If Your Spouse Needs to Go Into a Nursing Home?

This is a chapter we would prefer not to write. There are rarely happy endings and nursing home care usually takes a worse toll on the family than the patient. Regardless, this issue can't be ignored as we live longer and often need more care as we age.

On the other hand, based on what we usually hear from our clients, this chapter is really a wasted effort. That's because we hear the same solution over and over again when the topic of long-term care comes up. What do we hear? What's the solution? Pills. It's always the same: the wife will give me an overdose. The kids will give me an overdose. The dog will give me an overdose. They tell us they've already talked to them and they're all onboard. Right! Could this be the reason they keep building more nursing homes?

We suppose a disclaimer is in order. Most of our clients and the folks that we work with have built a nice nest egg. They're solidly middle class, not multi-millionaires. They worked hard, scrimped and saved to insure a comfortable retirement. Almost all our clients can fund a nursing home stay for at least three to five years without going broke.

What we've found is that about 25% of our clients have long-term care insurance (LTCi), versus about 7% of retirees across the country. Pretty good in comparison, but it still leaves 75% of our clients severely vulnerable to the increasing costs of long-term care.

We've already preached that retirees need a plan should they or their spouse need care. That plan may or may not include long-term care insurance, but there needs to be a plan.

What Does Nursing Care Cost and How Do You Pay for It?

In the Philadelphia market and most of New Jersey, we've found that nursing homes run an average of $7,000 to $9,000 per month. Yup, close to or a little more than $100,000 a year after the "extras." Maybe pills aren't such a bad idea?

Again, inflation is a big factor since health care costs of all sorts continue to rise faster than the rate of inflation. What retirees fail to do is take into consideration not just today's costs, but the future costs of long-term care 15 or 20 years down the road.

Impact Of Inflation On Nursing Home Costs

 You're 60 years old today and don't know if you should purchase long term care insurance. Figuring a nursing home in the Philadelphia area CURRENTLY averages around $100,000 per year including all costs, based on 5% inflation (based on history), that same care will cost $265,000 per year in 20 years when you might need care.

The easy part is finding out what nursing home care costs; how to pay for it is often quite complex, depending on the family circumstances. The purpose of this chapter is to give you an overview of the issues. Should you or a loved one need care, there is a counselor at each nursing home that will help guide you through the cost structure and Medicaid rules and regulations.

As we discussed in Chapter 4, if you are married, and your spouse needs to go into a nursing home, in Pennsylvania, your IRA is not subject to spend-down. Rules vary from state to state.

Again, we refer to the spouse who needs the care as the *nursing home spouse* and the stay at home spouse the *community spouse*. In

Pennsylvania, the IRAs and other qualified accounts of the community spouse are not subject to spend-down for the care of the nursing home spouse.

What's important to understand is that if you are married and if one spouse needs nursing home care, Medicaid does not want to put the community spouse into poverty. There are formulas used to calculate how much of the couple's money must be spent for care and how much is available to support the "at home" spouse.

If you are single, the rules are very different. Basically, you need to spend down to your last $2,000 before Medicaid kicks in to cover your needs. Not to worry, when you are broke the state gives you around $40 a month for all your incidentals.

Should We Save Ourselves and Self-Insure?
Many folks decide to self-insure. That's a plan, although not always a very effective plan. Let's take a 65-year-old couple just starting to get serious about long-term care, since one of their mothers is now in a nursing home. They ask us to run LTCi quotes. We tell them a decent policy will run $7,000 per year, for both husband and wife. They then tell us they'd rather just invest the $7,000 per year into a separate account earmarked for their long-term care. This is one of the stupidest plans we've ever heard.

Think about it: after 20 years, you would have stashed away $140,000. Let's assume a 5% growth rate. This account would have grown in value to $210,000 due to smart (or lucky) investing acumen.

With the long-term policy in this example, you would have started out with coverage of $180 per day for four years, or total coverage of about $525,000. In addition, this policy was purchased with a 5% compound interest rider, meaning the benefit grows and compounds at 5% per year until coverage is needed. So the daily room coverage goes from $180 the first year of the policy to $189 the second year and to $199 the third year. The overall protection you bought increased after one year from $535,000 to a little over $551,000. After 20 years, you and your spouse have a benefit value of $1,606,000 should you need care.

So think about it. Which sounds better to you; $210,000 or $1,606,000? Remember, this assumes neither will need care for 20 years. Suppose you need it tomorrow? Next year? The year after? You never know!

Bottom line, when many of our clients buy long-term care insurance, what they are really buying is asset protection. As much as their kids may drive them nuts, at the end of the day they need to decide whether they'd prefer to leave their money to the kids or the nursing home. Talk about a no-win decision!

What's Covered in a Typical Long-Term Care Policy?
Today most LTC policies allow benefits to be used for:
- Nursing Home Care
- Home Health Care
- Assisted Living Homes
- Adult Day Care

This is so important because most folks prefer to stay at home should they need skilled care. With the advances in medical technology, it's much easier to be cared for in your home.

Same goes for the choice between a nursing home and an assisted living facility. For many folks, assisted living is a much better option and saves a good few thousand dollars a month. Food's also better, so we're told.

Can I Give Away My Money Now?
Good question, and an easy answer is, it all depends. Up until 2005, there was what we called a "Three-Year Look Back," which basically meant you needed to give away your assets three years before you needed care. Otherwise, it was considered your money, and you needed to spend it for your care.

WHAT IF YOUR SPOUSE NEEDS TO GO INTO A NURSING HOME?

As part of the Deficit Reduction Act of 2005, the Three-Year Look Back became five years. President Bush signed the bill into law on February 8, 2006. No doubt the Deficit Reduction Act did the trick. Look Ma, no more deficit!

Why the time change from three to five years? Medicaid was (and still is) going broke. What was meant to help the poor had turned into another middle class entitlement program; Medicaid was paying for nursing home care it had never budgeted for. Too many folks gave away their money, gave their houses to their kids and otherwise took advantage of all the loopholes in the Medicaid rules.

Planning ahead five years is tricky. Who knows what their health will be that far in advance? In advance, retirees need to think long and hard before gifting their assets to the kids. We recently had a case where Mom put her house into her son's name. Guess who shortly thereafter found himself in divorce court? Guess who got half of Mom's house?

One rule to follow is to never put accounts or assets into your kids' names, if you'd never put those same assets into your son-in-law's or daughter-in-law's names.

There are some tools we can deploy for those that want to do some creative planning now to insure their estate is not subject to Medicare spend-down. Just know these techniques are tricky, and need the coordination of your financial planner and your elder law attorney.

Are There Any Other Options Besides Traditional Long-Term Care Insurance? Wouldn't you know it, there is one more option being used more and more today by those in decent health. Bet you can't guess? Yes – life insurance!

Today, many companies are offering combo life insurance-long-term care policies. Sometimes we refer to these policies as hybrids. The concept is this; you buy a whole life or universal life insurance policy that includes a long-term care rider. A portion of the death benefit can be used during your lifetime to cover some or all of your long-term care needs.

There are many hybrid policies on the market and they all work a little differently. For example, one company we work with allows you to pull out 95% of your death benefit during your life for long-term care needs. So let's say you had a policy with a death benefit of $600,000. You could take out up to 24% per year, or a total of $144,000 per year, for four years.

The policies I like are indemnity policies versus reimbursement policies. It's simple to get the funds for your care. Just have a doctor sign off that you are unable to perform two of the six activities of daily living (ADLs), and the funds are paid directly to you for use in a skilled nursing home, an assisted living facility or for home health care. No red tape and not a million forms to fill out.

Of course, after you have taken that last limo ride your beneficiaries would only get a total of $30,000, since you used up $570,000 in benefits to cover your long-term care costs. Pretty good deal!

Even better, if you die in your sleep at home one night and never needed long term care, your beneficiaries would get the full $600,000 at one time. Trust me, they will throw you one hell of a going away party, or as we call it today, a celebration of life. Only problem is you're not there to enjoy it, even though it was your life and you paid for it.

CHAPTER TEN

Building a Solid Estate Plan by Jeremy A. Wechsler, Esq.

Today you can go online or buy software to write a will. This is a real disservice to many people who later come to find that their estate plan is inadequate, incorrect, or both. That is, if they ever do find out! Chances are it'll be their kids or grandkids that will have to clean up the mess. I get calls all the time about severe conflicts and problems that all started based on a really simple will. Trust me, it can and does happen.

Doing estate planning by yourself is like being your own doctor. Sure, there's a chance your diagnosis will be correct. Maybe you'll prescribe the correct medicine. But how do you know for sure? I, for one, would never take such a risk. I could go online and look up my symptoms, but I am not a doctor, and didn't go to medical school for years. It's scary when *you don't know what you don't know!*

Doing estate planning correctly requires a full diagnosis—learning about your family, your needs, and your circumstances. Only then, can the correct plan be designed. Estate planning presents a series of issues, and every family is unique.

Here are just a few of the issues that could possibly arise, now or in the future:
- You become sick or disabled and need long-term care.
- Your child divorces and his or her spouse attempts to claim half of your estate.
- You don't get along with one of your children.

- You want to leave assets to grandchildren.
- You have several assets, all of which are titled differently and could cause problems later on.
- You have a blended family, as a result of second or third marriages.
- Your kids don't get along.
- Your kids are spendthrifts.
- You have a special needs child or grandchild.
- Your children are in high-risk professions, and could get sued as a result.

These issues are scary, and could cause problems with your estate plan in the future. Who knows what the future holds? We might have some idea based on the past, but we never truly know, do we? Furthermore, no one wants to ponder every possible scary outcome that could occur, or examine conflicts in their family that could present a problem later on. But at some point, there's going to be a time when these issues need to be addressed. You have the choice of addressing the challenges while you're engaging in estate planning, and finding solutions to the problems. Otherwise, you may leave your family with years of problems, conflicts, aggravation, and severed ties. Some folks that walk through our doors say things like, "I don't care what happens when I go," or, "I'll let my kids duke it out after I'm gone." My response is to ask if that's really the legacy they want to leave.

Let's pause briefly from the scary thoughts above. Ninety-five percent of all estates are settled peacefully and without conflict. I hope you fall within the 95%. But it's impossible to know what will happen down the road, and that's why it pays to make sure your estate is properly planned, with adequate thought given to the many issues presented above.

You a DO-IT-YOURSELFER?
The best estate planners start from the worst case scenario in the future and work back to the present. Be assured that a $39 software program or web site will not do that.

Instead, if you really want to tackle estate planning and build a solid estate plan, a consultation with a qualified estate planning attorney is probably the most important component of building your plan. Assuming you pick a qualified attorney, he or she will educate you about estate planning options and techniques. In return, you will educate the attorney about your family, circumstances, estate planning fears and goals, etc. That conversation will lead to a meeting of the minds and the design of a plan that works for you.

Do I Need a Will or a Revocable Living Trust?
This is a question that I hear daily, so you're not alone in being confused about what the right plan is. If you Google "Revocable Living Trust," you only get 528,000 results!

A will or living trust usually serves as the foundation of any estate plan. There may be other tools needed to craft your plan correctly.

A will is a death document—it's a one shot deal that distributes your assets upon your death. You can have standby trusts in your will, what we call testamentary trusts, for children and grandchildren. Those trusts aren't actually established until you die. A will must go through probate, which is the process of proving your will, having your executor formally named by the state, and advertising the estate to creditors in a local paper.

A living trust is a will substitute. You put your stuff (bank accounts, real estate, portfolios, etc.) into the trust during your life, and you keep complete control over the trust and the stuff in it over your lifetime. You designate successors to take over the trust duties, if you become disabled and unable to continue the task, and when you pass on. For any assets that were put in the trust while you were living, probate is avoided. To avoid probate, you must ensure that you put your stuff in your trust while you're living. Not everything goes in the trust—some assets have beneficiary designations that also avoid probate. But you

71

may decide that a large IRA may be best sheltered in a retirement trust, or a life insurance policy be owned by a life insurance trust. Later in this book, I'll talk about IRA Inheritance Trusts and the wonderful benefits they provide.

There's no perfect formula for deciding which foundational planning tool is best for you. However, I generally don't recommend living trusts for Pennsylvania residents, unless there are special situations.

Here are a few reasons why a living trust could be beneficial to you:
- You have property in multiple states. Shore house in NJ, home in PA, condo in FL? Then you might want to consider a living trust, because otherwise, you are potentially subjecting yourself to probate in three states!
- You want to ensure a smoother transition of your affairs to the next generation.
- You are worried about privacy for one reason or another, or have issues in the family where you're considering disinheriting a child or giving less to a child.

Many people also consider a living trust to avoid probate. Sometimes, this may make sense, but you should discuss this with your attorney before you make any decisions about whether to avoid probate. I talk more about probate in the next chapter.

Asset Protection Trusts for Kids and Grandkids
It's essential that you carefully consider how to structure a trust for a child or grandchild. Whether you use a will with a testamentary trust or a living trust, you must figure out how to balance the beneficiary's access to the trust fund versus asset protection.

Most people, if they make a concerted effort to leave an inheritance for a loved one, do not want to see it being spent- down unnecessarily by a spendthrift child or by a third party problem, such as a lawsuit, bankruptcy, divorce, etc.

Unfortunately, a lot of trusts are drafted without careful consideration of how to balance these two issues. We see a lot of faulty language in trusts that simply do not offer any protection to beneficiaries. I like to think of a trust like a tube of toothpaste: the stuff in the tube can only be squeezed out by the person who owns the tube. Hopefully, the beneficiary will only squeeze out of that tube of trust what they need, as they need it. That's because when that stuff has been squeezed out, anyone can make a claim on it. In other words, the more someone leaves in their trust the better we're able to protect it against creditors, bankruptcy, divorce, etc.

Some people are hesitant to restrict the inheritance for their children. I understand the fear of doing this, but always remember that anything you give to your kids is a gift that you didn't have to give in the first place! If you're giving this gift, why not do it in a way that protects your children from themselves and others? They may not be too happy finding out that they can't squeeze the entire tube of toothpaste out at once, but later on, they'll appreciate the fact that you created a safe haven for them.

Powers of Attorney: Priority Number One!
A will, as you know by now, is a death document. A living trust is also a death document, but also provides for the care and maintenance of the assets in the trust during your incapacity, and allows for assets to be held in the trust after your death. You need documents that always protect you and your affairs during incapacity. Otherwise court intervention will be needed (and no one wants that).

You *absolutely need* a power of attorney (POA), no matter which estate planning tool you have used. Even with a fully funded living trust, there are probably assets that go directly to beneficiaries; a POA is required to maintain those assets. Actually, you need two powers of attorney – a Durable Financial Power of Attorney and a Medical Power of Attorney.

These documents are accessible and relatively simple to draft, *but they still must be drafted carefully*, especially your durable financial power of attorney. We need to carefully consider your needs and family situation when designing gifting powers and powers over your IRAs and retirement plans. Unfortunately, those two powers are prone to abuse, as illustrated in the next paragraph.

Consider a common scenario—you're married with two kids. The kids have always gotten along growing up, but they don't see each other much these days. One child is doing well (we'll call him James) while the other is struggling; he was laid off over a year ago (let's name him John). John lives closest to you, so you name him as power of attorney. When he becomes power of attorney, he realizes that you gave him power to change the beneficiaries of your IRAs (who are James and John equally) without any restrictions. Two years after becoming power of attorney, John and his brother are not on speaking terms. John realizes that he can remove his brother James as beneficiary, and does so. I doubt James would be very happy about this, and this case will likely end up in court and take years to resolve. This could all be avoided by a carefully drafted power of attorney that limits or tailors the various powers that a person gets.

Yes, you need powers of attorney even if you are married and even if you have a living trust! They are also a must-have for couples with young children.

Finally, you must make sure they are revisited at least every five years to keep them from going "stale." Banks, hospitals, and the institutions that need the power of attorney documents are hesitant to accept old documents. First, the law changes, on average, every few years regarding the language used in these documents. Second, institutions are taking on liability by accepting older documents, so they won't accept documents if they are doubtful of your true and current intentions.

Updating Your Plan – Review, Review, Review!
A solid estate plan that you write now reflects the facts on the ground today. Nothing you write in your plan is written in stone.

As you know, things change in our lives. Think back 10 years ago. Where were you then? Did you have grandkids? Were you retired? Are you retired now? Time sure does fly, especially the older you get. Because our lives change on a regular basis, your plan must be reviewed every few years to ensure that the plan still fits the circumstances. I recommend a full review every three years.

Hopefully, your attorney keeps in touch with you to remind you to do this. At our office, we check up with people once a year to make sure things are goings smoothly and that nothing needs to be updated. Better safe than sorry.

A Few Common Mistakes and Ways to Avoid Them
In this section, I am about to touch on a few common blunders that folks make when engaging in estate planning. I can only hit the tip of the iceberg with these, but they are nonetheless important to consider and to be wary of:

1. **Co-Executors and Co-Powers of Attorney:** Be very careful about naming two or more people to serve simultaneously in one estate role, such as an Executor. Yes, if you have two kids, you want to treat them both fairly, but to be clear, the role of an Executor or any fiduciary is an administrative role and does not mean one child is getting more than the other! I liken these jobs to those of a CEO. If you're concerned about the person you appoint not doing the right thing, then that person is not the right person to choose in any capacity. Furthermore, other checks and balances can be crafted to ensure one person never has unchecked control. Why are Co-Executors a problem? Unfortunately, all too often the Co-Executors won't see eye to eye on one or two matters and the process of settling an estate will be held up. These conflicts are extremely common and

costly. Be careful and know there are better ways to go about solving the desire to treat everyone fairly.

2. **Gifting the Home for $1:** All too often, we see a parent sign away their home to a child for both probate avoidance and to get the asset out of his or her name, in case they go into a nursing home. Meanwhile, we also see what happens when that child, who now owns the home (and Mom or Dad still lives there), gets divorced or gets sued. The house is now on the table to be taken away. Yes, it does happen. Gifting the home like this is an awful strategy. I have no idea why it remains a popular idea.

3. **Not Considering IRAs and Retirement Funds When Planning Your Estate:** All too often, people don't understand that their IRAs and several other assets do not pass through their will. You may divide your assets three ways in the will, and forget that you only divided your assets two ways in the IRA. The point is, it's important to have a full picture when planning.

Summing It Up:

Estate planning without consideration of your unique circumstances can present many hazards to you and your family down the road. Why put you or your family through a messy ordeal when there are better options?

To build a solid estate plan, you need to make sure you work with a qualified estate planning attorney. The attorney should ask questions, many quite personal, about you and your family, to get a full picture of the dynamics. The attorney should then work with you to design a plan, laying out the pros and cons of your specific decisions. You should ask questions and make sure you understand your plan and how it works, now and in the future. Then, once you have a plan, make sure you review it on a regular basis. If you follow that formula, you'll be on the road to building a solid estate plan.

Wow…you are probably thinking that this was a very confusing chapter….but it's critical to see this through. Take your time and read this chapter carefully; then reread it a second time if need be. While it's not much fun thinking about your passing on, it's important to prepare for your heirs. Think about it this way…none of us get out of alive. I know you want to be sure your family will continue to be taken care of after you are gone.

CHAPTER ELEVEN
Understanding the Probate Process by Jeremy A. Wechsler, Esq.

What is probate? For one, it's a term that is used to scare people into crafting expensive estate plans. But probate is really just the administrative process of dealing with an estate upon one's death, from proving the legitimacy of a will to naming an Executor and distributing assets to beneficiaries.

That doesn't sound too scary, right? Actually, how scary it is depends upon within which state you live. In some states, such as Florida and California, probate is a much more burdensome process that requires court involvement. Court involvement requires the Executor to appear before a judge multiple times, with the court supervising every move, and thus requires hiring an attorney to spend a lot of time on the estate, making the attorney quite rich.

But if you live in Pennsylvania, probate happens at an administrative government office called the *Register of Wills* and, in most cases, the time spent at that office is relatively brief. I've been in and out in 15 minutes and assuming there are no challenges, thorny issues, or problems, you really don't spend much time there. When the will is deemed to be legitimate, the Executor takes his or her oath and the probate fee is paid to the county (depending on the county and size of the estate, the fee is usually between $200-$1,000).

At that point, the Executor is charged with carrying out his or her responsibilities, which are settling the estate and acting in the best interest of the beneficiaries. These responsibilities include such tasks as paying debts, expenses, taxes, funeral costs, selling and liquidating any assets, advertising the estate to creditors, and distributing assets to beneficiaries. The Executor also keeps the Register of Wills office informed of the status of the estate. The Executor is the fiduciary in charge of the estate at that point, and must be careful to ensure that the letter of the law is followed.

Often the probate process is straightforward. It is more straightforward when there are no disputes, the estate is solvent, and there isn't a long list of holdings and assets. If the estate is more complex, or there are disputes (or the possibility of disputes), the Executor will usually find it necessary and wise to hire an attorney.

Should I Avoid Probate in Pennsylvania?
We have people rushing into the office constantly because someone on TV or in a book told them in big bold letters, **YOU MUST AVOID PROBATE!** But about 25 years ago, Pennsylvania made the probate process a lot simpler. Even after hearing that probate is relatively inexpensive and easier in Pennsylvania than other states, there are still people afraid of probate who wish to avoid it. No one will hold a gun to your head and tell you that you must write a will and have your assets probated. But probate is certainly not as evil as it's made out to be.

What Assets are Probated and Which Ones Aren't?
If you write a will, any assets that pass through your will are going to go through probate. This does not include jointly held assets with the right of survivorship (a typical case would be a husband and wife who have both names on the property deed). It also doesn't include accounts with a beneficiary already designated on it (think about your annuity, pension, life insurance policy, etc.—those already have beneficiaries and therefore pass directly to those beneficiaries). Accounts with a payable on death (POD) or transfer on death (TOD) designation also do not go through probate. Finally, any assets held in a trust do not go through probate.

It sure sounds like a lot of assets today already avoid probate! But unless you have 100% of your assets avoiding probate, by titling them a certain way or putting them into certain types of accounts as listed above, your estate will have to go through at least some probate.

There's no hard and fast rule on whether you should attempt to completely avoid probate, but we have found that for many clients, that is difficult to achieve.

Reasons to Avoid Probate

There are some legitimate reasons why you might want to avoid probate:

1. **Possible Will Contest:** If you have disinherited a child, or given significantly less to one child, you may be subjecting your estate to a possible will contest. In Pennsylvania, you have the right to disinherit a child, but you must indicate your specific intention to do so in your will. But that still may not deter an angry child from attempting to challenge your will, whether it's legitimate or not. A creative lawyer will always find a way to make an argument, whether credible or not. So if you fall into this situation, you may want to think about avoiding probate. Why? Because the probate process makes your will public, for anyone to see. Basically, you are making it easier for someone to challenge your will, because now they have a copy of it to scrutinize very, very carefully. If you have a revocable living trust and it's completely funded to avoid probate, the trust document is not public because it does not go through probate. That's not to say a trust can't be challenged, because it can, but you're making it more difficult to challenge the estate. To get a copy of the trust, the person contesting it will probably have to hire an attorney and go to court, which could discourage frivolous litigation.

2. **Probate in Multiple States:** If you have property in multiple states, you may have to go through probate in each of those states. The prospect of going through probate in more than one

state can be extremely burdensome. It may be wise to establish a trust if you have property in multiple states.

Does Avoiding Probate Mean You Avoid Inheritance and Estate Taxes? NO!

Many people have been misinformed that by creating a revocable living trust, they can completely avoid federal estate taxes and Pennsylvania inheritance taxes. That couldn't be farther from the truth.

Back in the late '90s, living trusts were all the rage, because the federal estate tax exemption amount was so low that many families were potentially affected by the tax. Many were told that a living trust would simply avoid all of those taxes. WRONG. A living trust or a will with a testamentary trust could have possibly *reduced* the taxable estate for a married couple. But avoiding estate taxes completely? Hardly.

Pennsylvania inheritance taxes are not very burdensome, but they are still a factor. You can't prevent your loved ones from having to pay PA Inheritance Taxes whether you have a will or a living trust. The tax rates are currently 0% for spouses, 4.5% for children and grandkids, 12% for siblings, nieces and nephews, and 15% for all others. The only way to avoid PA inheritance taxes is by giving up control (i.e., gifting) of your assets while you're still living. You must live a year or longer, after the gift is made, to avoid the taxes.

Is it worth it to give up control over a significant amount of your assets while you're living, just so your relatives can save some money on inheritance taxes? I don't know, but I would caution you against engaging in gifting for the sole purpose of limiting or avoiding inheritance taxes. The cons usually outweigh the pros. You must talk with a qualified estate planning attorney before you make decisions such as these. Just because your neighbor, friend or relative gifted the house to their kids for $1 doesn't mean it was a good idea for them, and it may be a terrible idea for you.

Remember that the estate planning process is unique for every family. Even "simple" cases have varying and specialized needs. A good estate planning attorney figures out exactly what you need to protect you and your family. Talk to your attorney about the probate process. A qualified attorney should be able to give you an honest and detailed assessment about whether probate should be avoided in your case, or not.

Most importantly, don't procrastinate! I've met with folks in their 80s who have no estate documents. When asked why, they simply say they just haven't had time to get around to it. Go figure!

CHAPTER TWELVE
Don't Forget the Grandkids

Many clients who walk through my doors have grandchildren and often want to leave them a token gift. We can easily take care of that. Other times, they want to make sure they leave enough for their grandchild's college education, so their kids aren't burdened with those dreaded student loans. Trust me, I know, since I'm still paying mine! Finally, there are some clients who want to make sure their grandchildren are taken care of for life. Maybe leave a check for life from Grandma and Grandpa. Sounds great, but how do you do it?

We have three strategies for grandkids, but none of them technically count as gifts.

529 Plans
The first is helping with college by contributing to their 529 plans. This is a great way to put away money for the grandkids, have it grow tax free, and be available to help offset the crazy costs of college today. About the only item in our economy facing steeper cost increases than medical care is the annual college tuition increases along with room and board. College costs, year in and year out, increase faster than the rate of inflation. It's almost a crime.

Life Insurance... Again
The second tool we use is our old friend, life insurance. Did you see this one coming? At least I'm consistent.

Maybe you want to leave all your money to your kids? I can appreciate that. But if you are in good health, why not leverage some of your money now, and buy some life insurance that you can leave specifically for the grandkids? Concerned that they'll spend it all before they are adults? We'll help design a plan to insure the money goes a long way, often building a trust to insure the money doesn't fall into the wrong hands.

So while not technically gifting now, you are using tools to design programs that will gift after you are gone. I always see a sense of calm come over my clients after we deploy one or two of these scenarios.

Multi-Generational IRAs
The third tool I encourage you to use is to leave part of your IRA to your grandkids as a multi-generational IRA. What a great way to remember the grandkids, but an even better way for your grandkids to remember you!

If set up correctly, your grandkids will get a check from Grandma and Grandpa, every year, for the rest of their lives. Talk about a gift that keeps on giving. We often encourage our clients to segment off a portion of their IRAs for the grandkids. If there are no kids or grandkids, maybe use this technique for those nieces or nephews you actually hear from, other than right before their birthday. This is a way to leave the young ones not just an inheritance, not just a pension for life, but also a true legacy.

A few years back, one of my clients died. A few months later, I received a call from my client's son. He just found out that his mom had left his kids part of her IRA money, and even better, we worked it out for the grandkids to get their required minimum distribution check every year, on his mom's birthday. He was elated!

When I suggest this planning strategy, folks generally resist. I usually hear the same thing—I'll leave my money to my kids and they'll give it to the grandchildren. Sure they will, if they don't spend it all before they buy your headstone or before they die. As an aside, you might want to not only pre-plan the funeral, but also pay for it in advance just in case the kids decide to spend all your money before they get around to burying you.

Truth be told, many of my clients could take or leave their kids. But oh those grandkids: perfect angels and so sweet, brilliant and incredibly talented, besides. Geez, do they adore those grandkids, especially after they drop them back off to Mom and Dad.

Nobody wants to think about it but life gets complicated if your child dies first, leaving their joint assets, including your inheritance, to who? You guessed it, your favorite son-in-law or daughter-in-law. I know, this really makes you feel great, especially when you realize your nest egg may end up going to your son-in-law's new wife and her kids and grandkids. What if your kid is in a second (or third) marriage with step-kids to boot? Feel that headache coming on right about now?

So, you love the grandkids. You want them to remember you. Using a multi-generational IRA is the third technique we use to gift later.

Let's use an example to illustrate how we work with grandparents so they can help their grandchildren for life.

First, the Scenario:
Sally and Jim are each 70. They have several million dollars in assets and live rather frugally. They want to take care of their two grandkids, Jennifer and Sammy, who are six and 12, respectively. Last year, they decided to convert a $500,000 IRA to a Roth IRA because they didn't need those funds and wanted to provide a tax-free inheritance to their grandkids. They want to leave each grandchild half of the Roth.

Sally and Jim's Initial Plan:
Sally and Jim were told that gifting to their two grandkids for life would be easy. All they had to do was update their beneficiary designation

form to write in Jennifer and Sammy as beneficiaries on the Roth IRA. So that's what they did and in a few minutes they were done. Simple, right? Unfortunately, though their intentions were noble, there are problems with what just happened above. Keep reading.

What Seemed Easy May Be a Huge Problem

What appeared to be good intentions above might cause big problems and unforeseen issues down the road. Furthermore, by naming grandchildren, or anyone else for that matter, as a beneficiary, you are giving them full rights and control over the inheritance. That means they could cash out the Roth IRA upon your death. By doing that, the grandkids would lose out on the enormous growth benefit, or "stretch out" of the IRA.

Graph Value of IRA Inheritance Using Different Beneficiaries and Taking Only MRDs

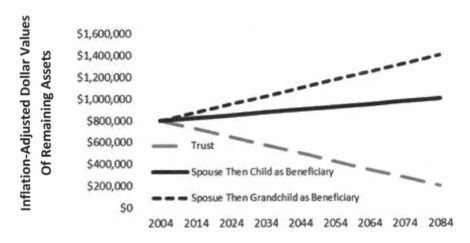

Upon your death, when the grandchildren receive their inheritance, the company that manages the IRA will send a form to the beneficiaries and ask them what they want to do with the account. One of the options will be to take a lump sum. In other words, Jennifer or Sammy could cash out their inheritance, and spend it all at once. If you're 21 years old, having the time of your life and need money, would you choose to hold the money in an IRA, which you've never heard of before, or take the money and run?

The Solution Is to Use an IRA Inheritance Trust:
Why not put the IRA into a trust? We call this type of trust an IRA Inheritance Trust. It's a special type of trust that must be carefully drafted by someone who understands how these types of trusts work. Why is it a special type of trust? The IRS is not interested in helping you preserve the wealth from your IRAs for future generations. By preserving the IRAs, you are delaying when Uncle Sam receives his tax dollars. We have to make sure the trust complies with several tricky IRS rules. But once you get through that hurdle, the trust is a beautiful device.

What Does the IRA Inheritance Trust Do?
The trust provides three significant benefits for your peace of mind—preservation, protection and enrichment.

1. **Preserve**: A trust ensures your grandchildren can't take that lump sum, and cash out the IRA all at once. This allows the IRA to grow over the lifetime of your grandchildren.
2. **Protect**: A trust is a treasure chest, and everyone loves a treasure chest. But, thankfully, you get to set the rules for who gets what from this treasure chest. We can build in restrictions for this trust, such as allowing the grandchildren to get a check every year for the required minimum distributions (based on his or her life expectancy). Or we may add in provisions that a trustee can distribute more than the RMDs for things like health or education.

   By building these restrictions in to the trust, we also do a good job of protecting the grandkids from themselves and from others. By doing this, the grandkids can't spend frivolously on that Harley Davidson or go on a shopping spree on Fifth Avenue. Instead, the IRA is there to help them over their lifetime—when they get married, when they have kids of their own and when those kids want to go to college. You can rest easy knowing the IRA will be there for those legitimate needs.

Protecting the IRA from creditors, predators, lawsuits, spouses, bankruptcy, etc. is also a key goal when building the trust.

The principle behind this type of asset protection is that the treasure remains in the chest. If the beneficiary can't take it, the creditors and predators can't either. Sure, if your grandchild owes child support and isn't paying, they can come after the treasure for that. But let's say your grandchild gets married and, a year later, is divorced. Should the spouse be entitled to half of the treasure? With the trust established, the spouse will have tough luck making his or her case on that one.

Contrast this with the initial plan above of putting Jennifer and Sammy on the beneficiary form which allows them to just cash out the IRA any time they wanted. If they did that, they would be exposing the entire IRA to creditors and predators.

Some of my clients want to think this will never happen. It's *unthinkable*. But consider a couple of facts:

- 50% of marriages in the USA result in divorce!
- There are millions (literally) of lawsuits filed every year in the USA. We are a litigious society.
- Our economy has been in a rut for the last decade, resulting in the housing mess we're in, people running up debt on their credit cards, and filing for bankruptcy. Oh, and what about the "lost generation"? These problems aren't going away anytime soon, and you want to ensure your grandchildren are, as much as you can help it, shielded from these realities.

3. **Enrich**: By ensuring that the IRA can grow over many years of the grandkids' lifetimes, you can enrich your grandchildren

much more so, than if they simply cashed out the IRA, blowing the money at once and/or exposing it to creditors and predators.

When Does the IRA Inheritance Trust Make Sense?
When deciding whether a trust makes sense, you should weigh several factors:

- Size of the IRA
- Number of beneficiaries
- Your estate planning goals, including your hopes and fears

There's no perfect formula, but for folks with large IRAs and young grandkids, the IRA Inheritance Trust makes a lot of sense.

Two last thoughts on the IRA Inheritance Trusts. First, they are good not only for your grandkids, but often for your kids also. Second, you need to make certain you are working with an estate planning attorney who understands the nuances of the IRS rules and can put together these trusts so they actually work as planned. You'll find not many attorneys know much about these trusts.

CONGRATULATIONS!

You have finished reading *Solving the Retirement Puzzle*. We hope that you found our book full of valuable information and great planning techniques. Our goal was to help you get started in solving your unique retirement puzzle. With so many pieces needing to fit together, the task can sometimes seem overwhelming. We've only scratched the surface in this book, and the next step will require your commitment to planning.

Don't procrastinate! Now it's time to build your action plan. Like most plans, the first step is the most crucial. So roll up your sleeves, do your research, and assemble the team that is just right for you.

It's never too early or too late to develop or modify a game plan that will help you protect your heath, your wealth and your family. Make sure you work with a team of retirement planning specialists. Their goals should be to ensure you have a long-term plan, never run out of money, and leave a well-crafted legacy plan for the next generation(s).

Our firm has been helping individuals and families solve the retirement puzzle for almost ten years and we love what we do. Let us know if we can help you solve your retirement puzzle.

ABOUT THE AUTHORS

The material presented in this book comes from the combined knowledge and experience of the authors, Peter and Jeremy Wechsler. This father and son team is dedicated to helping retirees, or those close to retirement, preserve and protect their assets, provide guaranteed lifetime income and to ensure that they have a customized, well-crafted legacy plan.

Peter Wechsler is a Registered Investment Advisor and president of Franklin Retirement Solutions since 2002. In his past life, Peter was president of Vend-Rite Service Corporation, a company he founded in 1971 at age 18. Peter was too young to retire after selling the company, and a few years later, he reinvented himself as a retirement & income planning specialist. In addition to his son Jeremy, Peter has been a foster dad and teen mentor for many years and is blessed to have seen his "kids" blossom in many fields.

Jeremy Wechsler is a licensed attorney in Pennsylvania, and his practice focuses on estate planning and elder law planning. After graduating from George Washington University, Jeremy taught in Philadelphia as part of the Teach for America program, while simultaneously earning a master's degree in education. Next, Jeremy graduated from New York Law School with an interest in estate planning. After graduation, Jeremy began his estates, trusts and elder law practice, helping individuals and families leave a well-crafted legacy plan and also plan for long-term care costs.

CONTACT US

Franklin Retirement Solutions
Peter R. Wechsler
Registered Investment Advisor
Your Retirement Quarterback®

Ph: (215) 657-9200 | www.FranklinRS.com | info@FranklinRS.com

The Law Offices of Jeremy A. Wechsler
Jeremy A. Wechsler, Esq.
Estate and Elder Law Attorney

Ph: (215) 706-0200 | www.JAWatLaw.com | info@JAWatLaw.com

2300 Computer Avenue
Suite J-54
Willow Grove, PA 19090

Investment Advisory Services offered through Brookstone Capital
Management LLC, an SEC Registered Investment Advisor.